LIBERWOCKY

WHAT LIBERALS SAY AND WHAT THEY REALLY MEAN

D1477694

VICTOR GOLD

WND BOOKS
A Division of Thomas Nelson Publishers
Since 1798

www.thomasnelson.com

Published in Nashville, Tennessee, by WND Books.

Library of Congress Cataloging-in-Publication Data
Gold, Victor, 1928-
  Liberwocky : what liberals say and what they really mean / Victor Gold.
    p. cm.
  ISBN 0-7852-6057-9
  1. Liberalism--United States--Humor. 2. Liberalism--United States--Humor--Dictionaries. 3. United States--Politics and government--Humor. 4. United States--Politics and government--Humor--Dictionaries. I. Title.
  PN6231.L47G65 2004
  423'.02'07--dc22

                              2004009520

Printed in the United States of America
04 05 06 07 PHX 5 4 3 2 1

* * *

To Barry Goldwater and Ronald Reagan
(who drove the Liberwocks nuts)

'Twas brillig and the slithy toves
Did gyre and gimble in the wabe;
All mimsy were the borogroves,
And the mome raths outgrabe.

"Beware the Jabberwocky, my son!
The jaws that bite, the claws that catch!
Beware the Jubjub bird, and shun
The fruminous Bandersnatch!

He took his vorpal sword in hand;
Long time the manxome foe he sought—
So rested he by the Tumtum tree,
And stood awhile in thought.

And, as in uffish thought he stood,
The Jabberwock, with eyes of flame,
Came whiffling through the tulgey wood,
And burbled as it came!

One, two! One, two! And through and through
The vorpal blade went snicker-snack!
He left it dead, and with its head
He went galumphing back.

"And hast thou slain the Jabberwock?
Come to my arms, my beamish boy!
Oh frabjous day! Callooh! Callay!"
He chortled in his joy.

'Twas brillig, and the slithy toves
Did gyre and gimble in the wabe;
All mimsy were the borogroves,
And the mome raths outgrabe.

—Lewis Carroll, "Jabberwocky,"
Through the Looking Glass

Make no mistake, at this relevant juncture in the history of our endangered planet the American mainstream looks to us for meaningful reform, a dramatic departure from the counterproductive policies of those who would turn back the clock at a time when, in the vision first articulated by John F. Kennedy ...

—LIBERWOCKY / ASSORTED SOUND BITES,
DEMOCRATIC NATIONAL CONVENTIONS, 1984-2000

CONTENTS

INTRODUCTION

THROUGH THE LIBERAL LOOKING GLASS

LIBERALS (ONCE YOU RESIST THE TEMPTATION TO take them seriously) can be a load of laughs. Think of those Nobel judges handing the 1994 Peace Prize to Yassir Arafat. Or Al Gore explaining how he not only invented the Internet but taught Tiger Woods everything he knows about addressing a golf ball.

Or consider the following excerpt from the *New York Times* of July 1, 2003:

> Ms. Kennedy-Cuomo, 43, said she fell in love with Mr. Cuomo, 45, when he took her on a tour of a homeless shelter on their first date and agreed to fast for the labor leader Cesar Chavez.

That would be Kerry Kennedy, she of the First Family of Liberalism, and Andrew Cuomo, the furrow-browed son of Mario, former governor of New York. Romance, Liberal-style . . .

He: What are you doing Saturday night?
She: What do you have in mind?
He: I thought maybe we could take in a movie.
She: A movie?
He: Or, better yet, a homeless shelter.

Obviously love at first blight: Begin with a drop-by at a camera-friendly homeless shelter. Follow with a solemn turn at the annual Cesar Chavez Fast-o-Rama. Finally, to seal the bond, a smoke-free dinner at the Four Seasons. Vegan, of course.

Hypocrites? Not in the double-standard orbit of the Kennedys and Cuomos. Preening gestures and vapid symbols have been the hallmark of modern American Liberalism from its Golden Age in the Kennedy-Johnson sixties to its thong-focused nadir in the Clinton-Gore nineties. Hand a hot-eyed Liberal an angst-driven placard . . .

SAVE THE AARDVARKS!

. . . and a march on Washington is all but assured (Jesse Jackson's schedule permitting). Not to mention the ritual add-ons we've come to expect from any Liberal Cause-of-the-Day:

Editorial outbursts by the *New York Times* and *Washington Post* excoriating "this administration's callous indifference to Nature Conservancy findings that the world's dwindling aardvark population is threatened with extinction by year 2030."

Full-page alarums in the *Times, Post,* and *Hollywood Reporter* paid for by the Malibu Committee for the Preservation of Nocturnal African Mammals (Janeane Garofalo, Chair).

A Ford-Foundation-sponsored PBS exposé ("Requiem for an Aardvark") hosted by Arianna Huffington, with simultaneous translation by Bill Moyers (consult your local TV listings).

Sound familiar? If you've come of age in the past half-century, it should. The cause may change and the add-ons mutate (remember "Hands Across America"?), but the Liberal m.o. doesn't vary, whether the placard reads . . .

PLUG THE OZONE HOLE!

Or:

FREE THE MEDELLIN SEVEN!

It's all of a piece once you've passed through the Looking Glass and entered into the obverse world of slithy toves, borogroves, and Liberal Jabberwocks.

> **"When I use a word it means exactly what I choose it to mean—no more, no less."**
>
> —HUMPTY DUMPTY, BEFORE THE FALL
>
> . . . .
>
> **"It depends on what the meaning of 'is' is."**
>
> —BILL CLINTON, BEFORE THE GRAND JURY

Not to get the Alice classics banned by the American Society of Politically Correct Pedagogues, but if Lewis Carroll were around today he'd be high on Hillary Clinton's hit list as a member of the Vast Rightwing Conspiracy.

Alice's creator was a conservative Oxford don with a jaundiced view of Liberals in general and Liberal Prime Minister William E. Gladstone in particular. Though written as children's stories, much of *Alice in Wonderland* and *Through the Looking Glass* is comic allegory aimed at Liberal cant, with Gladstone coming in for special treatment in the form of Alice's fustian friend Humpty Dumpty.

> "Now, take a good look at me! I'm one that has spoken to a King, I am: mayhap you'll never see such another: and to show you I'm not proud, you may shake hands with me!"

The leading Liberal of his day portrayed as a self-indulgent, egg-shaped windbag: Bill Gladstone meet Bill Clinton, Ted Kennedy, John Kerry. Some things in the quirky world of portside politics never seem to change.

But wait: Like a wayward guest at the Mad Hatter's Tea Party, I get ahead of myself. Definitions are in order. *Operative* definitions, as a Liberwock would say, since this is after all a book about words and their meanings.

> "The question is," said Alice, "whether you can make words mean so many different things."
>
> "The question is," said Humpty Dumpty, "which is to be master—that's all."

Exactly. No Liberal speechwriter in Campaign Year 2004 would see it otherwise. Ideas may have consequences (as Conservative scolds like Russell Kirk insist), but leave it to the Liberwocks to find a shortcut: Empty-calorie buzzwords that pass for ideas . . .

Liberwock. (1) A tunnel-visioned Liberal; (2) A member of an aberrant but pervasive political movement that flourished in the media-academic nexus of the United States during the latter half of the twentieth and early twenty-first centuries; (3) a Leftwing ideologue who stays up nights tormented by the thought that somewhere, somehow, a white middle-class American male might be enjoying life.

Liberwocky. The special jargon or code peculiar to this movement.

So you want to know what makes Liberals tick—or at least understand what Hillary, Ted, and other Liberals are driving at when they look into Katie Couric's inquiring eyes and utter mystic phrases like "meaningful dialogue," "chilling effect," and "Vast Rightwing Conspiracy"?

If so, you've come to the right book. Here, for the first time, you'll find the mystic veil lifted, questions asked that even Katie, in her relentless pursuit of truth-in-journalism, doesn't ask. Questions like:

Why do media outlets like *Time* and *Newsweek* identify blatantly Liberal think tanks like the Brookings Institution as benignly "non-partisan," while labeling Conservative think tanks like the Heritage Foundation "ultra-Rightwing"?

Why are outspoken Conservative leaders like Tom DeLay labeled "divisive," while outspoken Liberal politicians like Barney Frank are said to be "telling it like it is"?

Why is it that when Republican presidential candidates seek votes down South it's portrayed as a cynical, racist "Southern strategy," but when Liberals from Franklin Roosevelt to John F. Kennedy did the same they were simply mooring the Democratic "Solid South"?

But more, beyond Katie's limited realm:

Why is it that a Liberal avatar like Ted Kennedy has no problem calling himself a Liberal, without embellishment, while a Conservative president like George W. Bush feels it necessary to define himself as a "*compassionate* Conservative"?

Hmmm . . . You may, as Alice's bloviating friend Humpty might put it, puzzle over that one. But here's a hint: Words, like ideas—even empty-calorie words that pass for ideas—have consequences. Clearly a quizzical tour of the Liberwock mind is in order, a philologist's journey through the Liberal Looking Glass.

THE LIBERWOCK'S DICTIONARY

WHAT LIBERALS SAY AND WHAT THEY REALLY MEAN

A

AAUP (American Association of University Professors). In the theology of the political Left, the Liberal College of Cardinals. Note also **Democratic Leadership Conference (DLC),** the Liberal Curia Romana.

activist. A politically-concerned citizen given to the vigorous pursuit of Liberal causes. Not to be confused with **extremist,** a politically-concerned citizen given to the vigorous pursuit of Conservative causes (e.g., animal-rights *activist,* gun-rights *extremist).*

agenda, a.k.a. **hidden agenda.** As applied by Liberal conspiracy theorists (e.g., Gore Vidal, Norman Mailer), a clandestine plot by a Republican White House to suspend the Constitution, cancel all elections, and establish a government-by-junta. Note also **October Surprise.**

agrarian reformer. Liberal media characterization of China's Mao Tse-tung (1948) and Fidel Castro (1958) in response to simplistic Rightwing warnings that both were hardline Marxists who would establish dictatorial Communist regimes if they came to power.

alienated. Term used by Peter Jennings to describe Leftwing dissidents who take their grievances to the streets.

angry mob. Term used by Peter Jennings to describe Rightwing dissidents who take their grievances to the streets.

antiquated. Pertaining to that period of American history preceding the inauguration of John F. Kennedy, January 20, 1961. Note also **archaic, antediluvian, moss-backed.**

arch conservative, a.k.a. **ultra conservative.** As seen by the *New York Times*, any Conservative nominated to the federal bench by a Republican White House. Perceptive readers will note the absence of any comparable reference to **arch-** or **ultra-Liberals** in the *Times* style manual.

LIBERWOCKY

"I have been over into the future and it works."
—LEFTWING JOURNALIST LINCOLN STEFFEN ARTICULATING HIS LIBERAL VISION OF THE SOVIET UNION, 1920.

articulate a vision. Campaign trope favored by a generation of Kennedy imitators (e.g., Gary Hart, Bill Clinton, John Edwards). Invariably accompanied by a ten-point program and hundred-page White Paper outlining the candidate's solutions to problems we didn't even know we had.

artistic integrity. Creative Liberal's refusal to truckle to the crass commercial demands of a capitalist marketplace, choosing instead to pursue studies in Italy on a six-figure, tax-free grant from the National Endowment for the Arts.

TRULY STUPID LIBERAL IDEAS

Putting the U.N. in the U.S. Prime real estate, an ideal site for a new sports palace for the Yankees or Giants, but *nooo-o*, the Liberwock Rockefellers, guilt-ridden over their forebears' having left them all that money, had to offer up their feel-good contribution to the cause of World Peace. A grand gesture but guess who's left to pick up the tab half-a-century later?

Item: *The Washington Times*, February 4, 2004:

WHITE HOUSE SEEKS TO LOAN
U.N. FUNDS FOR RENOVATIONS

The Bush administration's new budget includes a $1.2 billion, thirty-year loan to renovate the aging United Nations headquarters and build a new annex, although U.N. officials expressed disappointment that Washington will charge interest on the loan.

B

bad judgment, a.k.a. **bad decision.** That which a Liberal politician says he exercised when caught accepting bribes, driving automobiles off piers, or engaging in sex with a young intern. Usually followed by a televised *mea culpa* in which he appears before voters in Armani-designed sackcloth to ask their forgiveness and understanding for having lost his moral compass. Note also **judgmental,** the refusal of a benighted constituency to forgive and understand.

balanced budget. Traditional Conservative obsession (discredited by John Maynard Keynes) *re* problems posed by government expenditures exceeding receipts. Oddly, though organizations like the *Washington Post-Newsweek* Corporation and the *New York Times* ardently support Keynes' enlightened view in government operations, they fail to see its merit in terms of their own business operations.

benign neglect. Term coined by Liberal U.S. Senator Daniel Patrick Moynihan to denote the quadrennial interest of Democratic presidential candidates in the plight of the inner-city disadvantaged. See also **ghetto-walking.**

LIBERWOCKY

bias. Warped, prejudicial slant on news coverage taken by Rightwing television reporters and radio talk-show hosts. In terms of **mainstream** reportage, nonexistent.

big government. Political entity whose "day" was officially declared "over" by Liberwock President Bill Clinton in his State of the Union message, January 1995. Nights are another matter.

bilingual education. By current U.S. educational standards, semi-literacy in two languages.

Brahmin, a.k.a. **Eastern-bred elitist.** In media coverage of presidential politics, label applied exclusively to George H. W. Bush, who was born in Massachusetts, attended Yale, joined Skull and Bones, and ran as a Republican; as distinguished from John Forbes Kerry, a Man of the People who was born in Massachusetts, attended Yale, joined Skull and Bones, and runs as a Democrat.

LIBERWOCKY

"I told her that at the end of the show I'd look into the camera and say, 'From the Right, I'm Robert Novak,' then she'd say, 'From the Left, I'm Margaret Carlson,' and she said, 'Oh, I can't say that! I'm middle-of-the-road.' What planet are these people living on?"

—CNN COMMENTATOR ROBERT NOVAK ON HIS EXPERIENCE BRIEFING *TIME MAGAZINE* COLUMNIST/CLINTON APOLOGIST MARGARET CARLSON FOR AN APPEARANCE ON CROSSFIRE.

LIBORIDDLE

Q. How many Liberals does it take to change a light bulb?

A. Fifty. One to change it, forty-nine to do the paperwork.

building bridges of understanding. Trade concessions to Communist China. Not to be confused with **constructive exchange,** i.e., foreign aid payoffs for Third World votes at the U.N.

bureaucrat. Your tax dollars inaction.

LIBERWOCKY

"What do you do at the Department of Interior?"

"I get off at four-thirty."

—ACTUAL DIALOGUE OVERHEARD ON
WASHINGTON METRO, AUGUST 2000

C

Camelot. A mythical Liberal era when all men were equal, affluent, and inspired, all women were beautiful, witty, and well-groomed, and *Republicans knew their place.* See also **U.S. government-in-exile.**

capital punishment. A crime. What, after all, would our world be like without Charles Manson applying for parole every three years?

challenging times. Yesterday, today, tomorrow. Liberal epistemology makes no provision for unchallenging times, since to do so would obviate the need for massive programs requiring substantial revenue enhancement.

chilling effect. That which cools the overheated ardor of biased Liberal journalists and educators. Word maven William Safire tracks the origin of this term to a 1965 Supreme Court opinion, but more likely it gained currency four years later when Vice President Spiro Agnew blistered the Liberal press establishment in a series of speeches penned by Rightwing troglodyte Pat Buchanan. (See following page.)

A FACEFUL
OF GARBAGE

WHEN SPIRO AGNEW MADE HIS BREAK-
through speeches exposing the bias of the eastern
Liberal media in the autumn of 1969 the reaction
was instant and predictable: The media, print and
electronic alike, first feigned shock, then struck
back with a vengeance.

Eric Sevareid, then the gray eminence of CBS
News (as well as a charter member of the Georgetown Liberal Establishment), said he felt as if he'd
been "struck in the face with a pail of garbage."
Liberal editorial writers and columnists outdid
themselves fearing for the future of the First
Amendment. Liberal cartoonists took turns depict-
ing Agnew as, variously, a Nazi Brownshirt and a
member of Hitler's SS. Beyond even the "chilling
effect," said Liberal alarmists, this effort by the
Nixon White House to "silence its critics" was only
a first step toward establishing the kind of
Rightwing dictatorship envisioned by Sinclair
Lewis in his cautionary novel *It Can't Happen Here.*

What Sevareid and other critics of Agnew

conveniently overlooked was the fact that months before the Republican vice president made those speeches, a House committee headed by Democrats had issued a report lacerating what it called "biased, sensational" television coverage of the 1968 Democratic convention in Chicago, where network cameras and commentators focused lovingly on Radical Left demonstrators protesting the Vietnam War.

That the House committee report was passed over as a non-event by the major news media should have come as no surprise. Over the years the Bigfoot editors, reporters, and commentators of the eastern Liberal media had set a limited agenda of what was and wasn't news fit to let the American people in on: The people's right-to-know filtered through the Liberal media's power to decide.

What that meant was that any story hinting at criticism of the media either hit the spike or was ignored altogether. Unless you'd just dropped in from Mars, you didn't hold your breath waiting for Mike Wallace to interview a House committee chairman about a report charging network bias or distortion in covering a story.

That was the standard. But a speech made by the

vice president, a man one heartbeat away from the Oval Office, couldn't be ignored. Like it or not, the Liberal media—the very "band of network commentators and self-appointed analysts" Agnew was exposing—had to cover it; after which, all hell broke loose.

On one hand, Spiro Agnew, until then depicted as Nixon's hapless, foot-in-mouth vice president, was transformed by the media into the worst menace to American freedom since Senator Joe McCarthy. But on the other, to the surprise of an appalled Liberal establishment, he became overnight the most popular vice president in American history.

Controversial, yes: Agnew drew high negatives in the public polls. But he also drew the highest approval rating of all the country's elected officials—higher even than the president's.

It was a message even the most insulated newspaper publisher and television news panjandrum couldn't ignore. And though Agnew himself would within a matter of years fall from the heights, he remains in Conservative memory the man who, whatever his Liberal critics say of him, first woke the American people up to the pervasive power of the Left-leaning media.

ON THIS DATE IN LIBERWOCK HISTORY

January 12, 1971: Harvard University offered its first accredited course in multicultural social studies, "The Deconstructive History of Discrimination in the Distribution of Street-Car Transfers in Johannesburg, South Africa," replacing ethnocentric "American History 101."

civil union. *The Odd Couple,* as written by Harvey Fierstein rather than Neil Simon. See also **uncivil union.**

closure. Mantric call, circa 1993-2000, for a statute of limitations on dialogue *re* presidential bimbo eruptions. Note also **move on** and **get it behind us.**

communism, a.k.a. **Evil Empire.** In Liberal memory, a spurious wedge issue exploited by radical Rightwingers to advance the political careers of Richard Nixon and Ronald Reagan.

THE IVY CURTAIN

"No, but I've been to Massachusetts."

—FORMER SECRETARY OF STATE JAMES A. BAKER III, RESPONDING TO A REPORTER'S QUESTION ON WHETHER HE HAD EVER VISITED A COMMUNIST COUNTRY, CIRCA 1980.

compassionate. Vote-getting descriptive fallen into Liberal disuse after being co-opted by ruthless, opportunistic Republican candidates.

conflicted. Low-grade Liberal Angst, generally applied to personal matters.

LIBERWOCKY

"If he wants to take money away from the aged, the blind, and the disabled, if he wants to take money away from poor women and children, I don't think so."

—COMPASSIONATE SENATE SENATOR JOHN BURTON (D-SAN FRANCISCO), ON BEING ASKED WHETHER HE'D SUPPORT GOVERNOR ARNOLD SCHWARZENEGGER'S PLANS FOR BUDGET CUTBACKS (OCTOBER 9, 2003).

complex. Liberal adjective describing problems with which Democratic administrations don't wish to deal (e.g., immigration, urban crime, any foreign policy crisis that requires more than sending Jimmy Carter to negotiate).

ON THIS DATE IN LIBERWOCK HISTORY

July 18, 1969: America learned to pronounce (if not spell) Chappaquiddick.

TRULY STUPID LIBERAL IDEAS

District of Columbia statehood. The idea here is to convert a dysfunctional, pothole-ridden city into a dysfunctional, pothole-ridden state. Question: Would statehood for the nation's capital not only fill the potholes but upgrade one of the worst (albeit best-financed) school systems in the country, reduce the crime rate, and otherwise improve the quality of life for Washington residents? Answer: No, but what difference does that make as long as it gives the Democrats two additional seats in the U.S. Senate?

A better option? If, as D.C. statehood proponents argue, Washington voters are entitled to two U.S. senators, simply cede the District back to Maryland. (Or aren't Maryland's two Democratic senators Liberal enough for them?)

Also, **Puerto Rican statehood.** The other side of the Stupid Statehood coin, this one derived from Republican Liberwocks running for president who, in pursuit of a handful of convention delegates, quadrennially promise to push for Puerto Rico as the fifty-first state.

And what, precisely, is wrong with that idea? Simply that Puerto Rico is a foreign country, the majority of whose citizens think of themselves, culturally and otherwise, as separate-and-distinct from the United States (apart from those Puerto Ricans who move to the mainland). Think not? Just check the Puerto Rican cheering section at the next Pan American games. They not only root against the *norteamericanos* when the mainland team is playing Puerto Rico, but when it's playing any other national team south of Miami (including Cuba)!

Conservative. Mild Liberal epithet for Rightwing opponents. Less mild are **Reactionary, Know-Nothing,** and **Crypto-Nazi,** applied by hyper-Liberal Gore Vidal to William F. Buckley in a televised debate during the Vietnam War. Note also **Fascist!**

Constitution. As interpreted by the Warren Court (1954-70), *an enlightened fount of freedom created by the revered Founding Fathers;* but as interpreted by the Burger/Rehnquist Court (1970-), *an outdated instrument of juridical repression promulgated by a clutch of eighteenth-century slaveholders.*

criminal. A dysfunctional victim of economic deprivation, childhood trauma, and/or societal neglect on the part of an insensitive political power structure and woefully underfunded state welfare system. Not to be confused with **White-collar Criminal,** a predatory crook. (For an especially **judgmental** use of the term, see below.)

LIBERWOCKY

"The dropping of the atomic bomb on Hiroshima was the most *criminal* act in the history of the world."

—REV. JESSE JACKSON, MASTER OF NUANCE, SAN
FRANCISCO, AUGUST 7, 1985

D

dirty tricks. Rotten, unethical, illegal campaign tactics employed by win-at-all costs Republican presidential candidates (e.g., the Nixon Gang, both Bushes). Not to be confused with **hardball,** the boys-will-be-boys tricks used by Democratic campaigners (e.g., the Johnson White House ordering an FBI check into the sex lives of Barry Goldwater's staff in 1964; Mayor Richard Daley's holding up the Chicago vote count until he knew how many would be needed to carry Illinois for Kennedy in 1960).

discrimination. That which occurs when two applicants for one position are equally qualified and the selection is based on race alone. Not to be confused with **affirmative action,** i.e., when two applicants for one position are equally qualified and the selection is based on race alone.

disenfranchised. Voters not represented by members of the Democratic Party. See also **Florida!,** along with Michael Moore's definitive diatribe on the problem: *I Voted Twice and Gore Still Lost!* (Cook County Press).

diversity, a.k.a. **multiculturalism.** Racial profiling as practiced by the Politically Correct. Note also as a Liberwock substitute for the retro concept of America as a melting-pot, the uplifting term **gorgeous mosaic,** favored by New York politicians (e.g., Mario Cuomo) when pandering to ethnic blocs during the 1980s and 90s. For another perspective, note history of Serbia, Bosnia, Croatia, Kosovo, 1200 A.D. to present. (See ad on following page.)

divisive. Pejorative applied by Democrats to every Republican president since Abraham Lincoln, more recently leveled by the Great American Unifier Edward Moore Kennedy in a 2003 speech accusing George W. Bush of duplicity, mendacity, and wartime "fraud."

dunce, a.k.a. **amiable dunce.** Liberal depiction of all but one Republican president in the past half-century. (See "Presidental Libofiction" on page 42.)

RENT-A-GUEST

*Embarrassed At Your Last Wine & Brie
Party When You Looked Around The
Room And Saw It Was Lily-White?*

We bet you were. It's an awful feeling. You probably stayed up half the night, torn by guilt pangs and resolved the next morning never to let it happen again.

In fact, you'd like to make amends by throwing another Wine & Brie soiree with the proper mix in order to salve your conscience and impress your Liberal friends.

But how? You've spun through your social Rolodex and discovered—horror of horrors—that you really don't have any African American, Latino, Asian, or Native American acquaintances you'd want in your home!

Quite a dilemma, but don't panic. That's where Rent-a-Guest enters the picture. As the oldest, most reliable guest rental service in the world, we've been solving social diversity problems for party-givers from the Hamptons to Beverly Hills, since 1963.

Some random testimonials from our select clientele:

"Al and I had planned this Earth Day picnic with a global motif and at the last minute discovered we'd come up short on the aboriginal front. How they did it I'll never know, but on one day's notice Rent-a-Guest produced no fewer than two Bantus and three Maori tribesmen to fill out our guest list."

—Tipper Gore

"With regard to African-American celebrity invitees I especially like Rent-a-Guest's policy of sending along two, in case the first one doesn't work out."

—Barbra Streisand

Interested? If you're a politically-attuned climber in Washington, New York, or Los Angeles, you ought to be. Why spend countless hours fretting over the proper mix at your social functions when all you have to do is—

CALL 1-800-DIVERSITY FOR ALL THE ANSWERS TO YOUR NEW YEAR'S EVE/SUPER BOWL/EARTH DAY PERSONNEL NEEDS*

RENT-A-GUEST: AN OFFICIAL EQUAL-OPPORTUNITY SUPPLIER

*BE SURE TO ASK FOR OUR SPECIAL ELECTION YEAR
RATES ON SAME-SEX MINORITY COUPLES AND
VERTICALLY-CHALLENGED PEOPLE OF COLOR.

PRESIDENTIAL LIBOFICTION

COUNT ON TWO THINGS WHEN LIBERALS LOSE a presidential election: (1) They'll put in a "foul" claim (see **dirty tricks** and **Florida!**) (2) They'll follow up trashing the process by trashing the winner, for example:

LIBOFICTION: Eisenhower was a syntax-challenged dimwit who blundered his way to victory in Europe during World War II and didn't have a clue about what was going on in a White House run by his military-industrial aides.

FACT: As borne out by independent historian Fred Greenstein in *The Hidden Hand Presidency*, Ike was one of the most deeply-involved presidents in modern U.S. history, smart enough to stop the shooting in an Asian land war that his Liberal predecessor had put us into, shrewd enough to keep us out of an Asian land war that his Liberal successor would get us into.

LIBOFICTION: Jerry Ford was an affable, uncoordinated buffoon who stumbled up the ladder to the White House.

FACT: Jerry Ford, the most athletic U.S. president since Theodore Roosevelt, was an honors student-athlete at the University of Michigan who might indeed have played football without a helmet (as Lyndon Johnson once sneered) but had brains enough to bring American troops home from the Southeast Asian killing field Johnson sent them into.

LIBOFICTION: Ronald Reagan, in the smirking phrase coined by Clark Clifford at a Georgetown gathering of the Liberal elite, was an "amiable dunce," an opinion shared by then-Speaker Tip O'Neill, who never failed to tell reporters that "All Reagan can do is read cue cards."

FACT: Clifford's "amiable dunce"* won two terms as governor of the most populous state in the Union and two terms as president—so what does this say about the street smarts of his Liberal opponents? As president, Reagan should be remembered (whether the Nobel Prize committee agrees or not) as the global strategist who, against all "expert" opinion (including Tip O'Neill's), faced down Gorbachev at Reykjavik and hastened the collapse of the Evil Empire—without a bomb being dropped or an American life lost.

---

*Historical endnote: In 1993 Clifford was indicted as a co-conspirator for having served as a frontman in what was called "the biggest bank fraud on record." Clifford's defense? He had no idea what was going on! Because of the defendant's age and health, a charitable U.S. District Attorney didn't prosecute, thereby saving an amiable Liberal dunce from a possible prison term.

LIBOFICTION: "Poo-o-or George" Bush, as Liberal den mother Ann Richards referred to the then–vice president at her party's 1988 national convention. Why "poor"? Because, according to Democratic conventional wisdom, George H. W. Bush was hopelessly burdened by what *Newsweek* magazine called "The Wimp Factor."

FACT: Try as they might to depict George the Elder as a bumbling, effete ex-Yalie more attuned to "The Whiffenpoof Song" than "The Eyes of Texas," Richards and the editors of *Newsweek* couldn't get around Bush's well-known history as a Navy aviator and hero in the Pacific in World War II or the fact that their own candidate, Michael Dukakis, was the pluperfect Harvard Yard Wimp, a mannequin posing as a warrior, perched for the cameras atop an armored tank, half-swallowed in an oversized helmet. Finally we arrive at the signal case of George the Younger—but let's hear poo-o-or Ann Richards (or her Texas helpmate, Molly Ivins) try to explain how, with all her Austin smarts, she managed to blow her governorship and pave the way to the White House for yet another clueless—if amiable—Republican dunce?*

---

*Oh, yes—the one exception: Richard Nixon, of course. Mephistopheles has been called many things, but never a dunce.

E

Emperor has no clothes. Liberwock parable exposing the mindless hypocrisy of American culture. According to the story, everyone compliments the parading Emperor on his raiment except one obstreperous boy (presumably a member of the Howard Stern Fan Club) who insists His Highness is naked. Note, however, that in recent years a revisionist version (advanced by a prominent Massachusetts senator) raises the question of whether the boy isn't actually one of seventeen million myopic American students who, as a result of health-care cuts by the Bush administration, can't afford corrective surgery by a competent eye doctor.

enabler. Granola Belt psychobabble for one who assists an alcoholic or sexually predatory associate **in denial.** (For a more positive spin on this New Age Liberal term, see below.)

LIBERWOCKY

"I am running for president of the United States to enable the goddess of peace to encircle within her reach all the children of this country and all the children of the world."

—REP. DENNIS KUCINICH (D-OHIO), ANNOUNCING HIS PRESIDENTIAL CANDIDACY IN CLEVELAND, OCTOBER 13, 2003.

entitlements. Beatified government handouts.

ethnocentric. *Re* arrogant, exclusionary Euro-American chauvinists, not to be confused with . . .

ethnic pride, reflected by culturally-awakened minorities responding to the identity crisis in their indigenous ghetto communities.

E Unum Pluribus, translation "Out of one, many." Latin uttered by then–Vice President Albert Arnold Gore while bloviating, circa 1995, on *his vision for America's future* before a claque of White House reporters. They let it pass, but would they have done the same if, for example, Dan Quayle had said it?

Washington Post, July 2, 1991

OUT OF ONE, MANY?
FOOT-IN-MOUTH QUAYLE DOES IT AGAIN
BY ROXANNE ROBERTS

PHILADELPHIA, PA—Vice President Dan Quayle added yet another howler to his collection of verbal missteps yesterday, this time in—of all languages—classic Latin.

Addressing an audience of visiting scholars at historic Independence Hall, the vice president somehow managed to mangle one of the country's most venerable maxims, "E Pluribus Unum"—translation, "Out of Many, One"—in a way described by one member of the audience as "hilarious if it weren't so pathetic."

Quayle, whose previous problems with the language include misspelling the world "potato" in an appearance at an elementary school, put even that episode in the shade last night in a rambling half-hour speech commemorating the 215th anniversary of the Declaration of Independence.

Departing from his advance text, the vice president, wearing an ill-fitting blue Brooks Brothers suit with inappropriate brown loafers, cited the Declaration as representing "the coming together of America's thirteen colonies in a spirit of one for all, all for one—E Unum, Pluribus!"

That is—as even a grade-school student of Latin should know—"Out of One, Many," a blooper-of-bloopers that led one embarrassed Quayle staffer to shake his head and comment, "For a guy with a double-digit handicap in English, you'd think he'd have sense enough to stay away from Latin . . . "

evolve, a.k.a. **to grow.** To move politically from Right to Left, as when Robert F. Kennedy transmuted from Joe McCarthy acolyte in the 1950s to Liberal paladin in the 1960s.

LIBERWOCKY

"I am a former Rightwinger who has evolved into a compassionate and progressive populist."

—ARIANNA HUFFINGTON ON HER FAVORITE SUBJECT
(ARIANNA HUFFINGTON), SEPTEMBER 2003

F

family values. Rightwing code words *re* qualifications to look for in presidential candidates. (For a Liberwock perspective on subject, see below.)

WARREN BEATTY FOR PRESIDENT?

"You're much more likely to find great leadership coming from a man who likes to have sex with a lot of women than one who's monogamous."

—POLITICAL ANALYST/ FILM STAR ETHAN HAWKE,
QUOTED IN DETAILS MAGAZINE, MARCH 2004

Fascist! A card-carrying, Limbaugh-listening member of the National Rifle Association who votes Republican, smokes in restaurants, and drives a gas-guzzling SUV.

flip-flop. Simplistic Rightwing label applied to a discerning Liberal's agonizing reappraisal of a previously-held position, e.g. John Kerry's switching sides on the Iraq War issue after "thoughtful political consideration" (*New York Times* Letters, March 6, 2004). See also **waffling, zigzag.**

Florida! Democratic rallying cry, reflecting bitter memory of the 2000 election being arbitrarily decided by the 5-4 vote of a Republican Supreme Court when (by all rights) it should have been equitably decided by the 5-0 vote of a Democratic state Supreme Court.

Fox News. First ax in the Rightwing Axis of Evil. Note also **Rush Limbaugh, Matt Drudge.**

freedom of speech, a.k.a. **First Amendment rights.** As interpreted by the U.S. Supreme Court, the right to burn the American flag on public property as long as it isn't done as part of a church-related ceremony.

ON THIS DATE IN LIBERWOCK HISTORY

May 11, 1968: First-year Yale law student Hillary Rodham got an A-minus in Legal Ethics.

THE FIRST FIFTY LIBERWOCKS*

EXTRACTED FROM THE DEFINITIVE SOCIAL awareness Register, *Who's Lib in America*, published annually by People for the American Way (Lear Press). Previous (2003) ranking in parentheses.

1. Hillary Rodham Clinton (1)
2. Ted Kennedy (3)
3. John Kerry (17)
4. Al Franken (42)
5. Bill Clinton (2)
6. Tom Daschle (6)
7. Nancy Pelosi (12)
8. Katie Couric (8)
9. Peter Jennings (7)
10. Martin Sheen (13)
11. Dan Rather (14)
12. Barbra Streisand (12)
13. Eleanor Clift (15)
14. Al Gore (4)
15. John Edwards (unlisted)
16. Barney Frank (11)
17. Henry Waxman (27)
18. Michael Moore (43)
19. James Carville (19)
20. Alec Baldwin (23)
21. Al Sharpton (26)
22. Paul Begala (21)
23. Gore Vidal (20)
24. Jesse Jackson (11)
25. Bill Maher (24)
26. Rob Reiner (47)

---

* Numbers current as of June 30, 2004. Rank subject to change by cybervote@lib.net.

27. Tom Brokaw (31)

28. (tie) Norman Lear (18)

28. (tie) Ted Turner (18)

29. Gloria Steinem (28)

30. Susan Sarandon (27)

31. Charles Schumer (36)

32. Tim Robbins (29)

33. Jane Fonda (35)

34. Matt Lauer (37)

35. Paul Krugman (unlisted)

36. Arthur Schlesinger Jr. (34)

37. Chris Dodd (41)

38. George McGovern (33)

39. Molly Ivins (21)

40. Pat Leahy (47)

41. Patty Murray (49)

42. Bill Moyers (38)

43. Barbara Boxer (22)

44. Mario Cuomo (44)

45. John Conyers (40)

46. Jimmy Carter (25)

47. Bono (unlisted)

48. John Corzine (49)

49. Janeane Garafolo (48)

50. Margaret Carlson (50)

G

gender gap. Liberal media conundrum first posed by a bored desk editor at the *Sacramento Bee*, circa 1980, viz. (1) the inability of the Republican Party to get wives to vote like their husbands; (2) the inability of the Democratic Party to get husbands to vote like their wives.

ghetto-walking, a.k.a. **campaign slumming.** Showhorse touring of inner-city neighborhoods, a Liberal vote-trolling technique developed by Senator Robert Kennedy and New York Mayor John Lindsay in the mid-1960s, since abandoned after complaints by ghetto-dwellers that "after the cameras leave, nothing happens."

global warming. Intimations of worldwide catastrophe based on a beastly warm ski-season in Aspen. See **Al & Tipper's Horrible Vacation.**

ON THIS DATE IN LIBERWOCK HISTORY

April 20, 1957: An acorn fell on young Al Gore's head, and he rushed into the house to tell his mother the sky was falling.

TRULY STUPID LIBERAL IDEAS

The World Court, a.k.a. **The International Court of Justice.** Fifteen judges, some drawn from such justice-loving nations as Libya, Iran, North Korea, Zimbabwe, and Cuba, all elected to nine-year terms by the U.N. General Assembly and Security Council. Should the United States submit its citizens, not to mention its national interest, to fiats handed down by such a court? The Liberwocks think so. Bill Clinton, in one of his last acts in office, went so far as to sign the treaty; though needless to say it wasn't ratified by the Rightwing xenophobes in the U.S. Senate who, predictably, questioned the impartiality of the judges.

Baffling. After all, don't they have the reproachless record of international judging at the Olympics to reassure them?

Granola Belt. That strip of Liberal territory running from northern California to the Canadian border and inhabited by Eddie Bauer-wearing, tree-hugging pseudo-naturalists who characterize themselves as Greens.

greatness. Liberal idea of what every American chief executive should aspire to, as borne out by Bill Clinton's post–White House regret that there hadn't been a war during his tenure because, he said, "if there had been, I'd have gone down as a great president." (For another presidential point of view, see below.)

KEEP COOL WITH CALVIN

"It is a great advantage to a president and a major source of safety to the country for him to know he is not a great man."

—PRESIDENT CALVIN COOLIDGE ON HIS DEMOCRATIC PREDECESSOR, WOODROW WILSON.

guilt. Given the Liberal premise that all crime is society's fault, a medieval concept irrelevant to modern times. See **root cause.**

guilt by association. Rightwing Republican technique of impugning the reputation of a political opponent by smear and sly innuendo. (For straightforward rejection of this technique by a Liberal Democratic leader, see below.)

"THAT WOULD BE WRONG"

"You can practice guilt by association, but I think that would be wrong.

"I think it would be wrong to say that of any-one, you know, of Senator Dole because his chief financial advisor went to prison, I don't think that—does that mean that Senator Dole did wrong? I'm not sure. I don't think it does."

—BILL CLINTON, MAKING IT PERFECTLY CLEAR THAT HE DOESN'T BELIEVE BOB DOLE SHOULD GO TO PRISON.

gun control. Liberal interpretation of the Second Amendment that restricts the citizens' right to bear arms to those who bear them in order to carry out criminal acts.

LIBERWOCK PLEA OF "NOT GUILTY"

"I haven't committed a crime: What I did was
fail to comply with the law."

—FORMER NEW YORK MAYOR DAVID DINKINS
RESPONDING TO QUESTIONS RAISED ABOUT
HIS FAILURE TO PAY HIS INCOME TAX.

H

Halliburton. Red meat for the Liberwock soul.

hate crime. Criminal conduct that finds the perpetrator carrying out his assault, robbery, or murder harboring biased thoughts about his victim's race, religion, or sexuality. Not to be confused with mere **crime,** in which the perpetrator carries out his assault, robbery, murder on an equal-opportunity basis.

healing. In Liberal theology, pain-free absolution.

LIBERWOCKY

"This is a time for healing and forgiveness."

—CLINTON ATTORNEY ROBERT BENNETT,
LIBERWOCKING ON BEHALF OF AN EAST
EUROPEAN DIPLOMAT BEING HELD ON DUI
FOR RUNNING OVER AND KILLING A YOUNG GIRL.

history (American/European). By current standards of the **American Association of University Professors,** a non-essential subject of ethnocentric origin best replaced in college curricula by core studies in postmodern community life (e.g., *The Role of Gender in Extra-Marital Relations between Consenting Species*). But note also the . . .

History Channel. A cable outlet dedicated to edifying documentaries featuring little-known historical facts (e.g., that Richard Nixon, J. Edgar Hoover, Lyndon Johnson, and Lee Harvey Oswald dined together at a Dallas restaurant the night of November 21, 1963, to plot the assassination of John F. Kennedy).

HUAC. Rightwing bogeyman invoked by Liberal mothers to shush their squalling infants, circa 1940-55. Assailed for having launched Richard Nixon's career in the infamous hounding of Alger Hiss. Note also **red herring, witch hunt.**

TRuly StuPid LiBeRAL idEAS

The Twenty-fifth Amendment. If the law of unintended consequences ever played out, it was the August day in 1974 when Jerry Ford, who had become president under the terms of the Twenty-fifth Amendment, made Nelson Rockefeller his vice president, thereby creating—for the first time in American history—a national administration led by not one but two unelected officials.

How did it happen? Start with the amendment's chief sponsor, a helium-headed Liberwock senator from Indiana, Birch Bayh (whose son Evan now sits in the same Senate seat, a Liberwock dynasty in the making). After the assassination of John F. Kennedy in November 1963, Bayh the Elder felt the urge to do something about Lyndon Johnson's serving in the Oval Office without a vice-presidential backup.

Why anyone should think the country needed a vice president at the time is hard to say. The Constitution clearly provided a line of succession behind Johnson, beginning with the Speaker of the House. But Bayh pressed on, and by sheer Hoosier persistence moved his unneeded amendment* through both houses of Congress and the requisite number of state legislatures to become law of the land.

But wait. Back up and ask the question: What would have happened in 1973-74 if there had been no Bayh Amendment, and first Agnew, then Nixon had resigned? Simply this: Nixon's resignation without a vice president in place would have elevated House Speaker Carl Albert to the presidency. By 1976, two years of Democratic control of both the White House and the Congress would have made Watergate a non-factor in a presidential race between either Albert or Jimmy Carter and his Republican opponent, Ronald Reagan, the former California governor who almost certainly would have defeated House minority leader Gerald Ford for the Republican presidential nomination. Reagan would have been elected, there would have been no national "malaise" or Tehran hostage crises in the late seventies, Elvis Presley wouldn't have died in August 1977 . . .

Ah, but there I go, drifting into the Liberwock trap, a fool's-gold vision of the perfect world.

---

*For that matter, has any constitutional amendment since the Fifteenth—other than the Nineteenth and Twenty-fourth—really been needed?

I-feel-your-pain. (1) Political Oprah-ism. (2) An empathoid phrase, conveying synthetic empathy, contrived (with accompanying hug) by Bill Clinton, 1992-1996. Note also an earlier line that connected with a gullible public, **I'll-never-lie-to-you** (Jimmy Carter, 1976).

illegal alien. Exclusionary term applied by early twentieth-century jingoists to geographically dislocated inhabitants. See also **undocumented**.

implacable. Also **hard-line, last ditch, old guard.** Pertaining to **Rightwing zealotry;** as contrasted with **resolute, principled,** mainstream media's characterization of Liberal implacability.

in denial. Liberal psychobabble used in argument when all else fails. (For inspired use of the concept, if not the term by an ACLU spokesman, see facing page.)

Lawyerwocky

infidelity, a.k.a. **adultery.** In sexually Liberated households, mere marital outsourcing.

infrastructure. Roads, bridges, tunnels, waterways in dire need of robust upgrading to meet the growing challenge of the New Economy's post-industrial paradigm, i.e., election-year boodle for Congressional incumbents. For the definitive work on the subject, see West Virginia Senator Robert Byrd's two-volume work, *If It Moves, Pave It* (Pork-Barrel Press, Charleston).

insensitivity. White male college editor's inability to empathize with African-American student rage that led to trashing his office and burning all editions of an issue featuring material they deemed "racist."

"is". Regarding whose meaning, in the view of America's forty-second president, it all depends. For further study of this semantic conundrum, see I. A. Richards' seminal *The Meaning of Meaning* (Oxford Press).

J

jingoist. (1) One who wears an American-flag lapel pin to a meeting of the Boston Council on Foreign affairs; (2) A Stetson-hatted Texan who orders California Pinot Noir on an Air France flight to Paris.

judgmental. Draconian Rightwing response to wrongdoing despite the wrongdoer's abject public apology, plea for a second chance, prayer for spiritual guidance, and promise to (1) give back the money or (2) pay child support.

GOD'S UNFINISHED WORK

Accused of anti-Semitism for having referred to New York City as "Hymie-town," Reverend Jesse Jackson in 1984 apologized to Jewish leaders by explaining that "God is not finished with me yet." Seventeen years later, Jackson (obviously one of God's long-term projects) announced he would be "taking some time off to revive my spirit and reconnect with my family" when news broke that he'd fathered a child out of wedlock and used foundation funds to pay off his paramour. See also Bill Clinton's revision, "Character is a journey."

Judgment of History. Factitious verdict handed down by a stacked jury of Liberal revisionists bent on redeeming the reputation of failed Democratic presidents.

SPIN-DOCTORING HISTORY

EVERY DECADE OR SO A SELF-ANOINTED PANEL of what the *New York Times* chooses to call "distinguished historians" confects a list purporting to rank American presidents as Great, Near-Great, Average, and Worst.

The results are invariably the same: Washington, Jefferson, Jackson, Lincoln, Franklin D. Roosevelt, and Wilson are ranked as Great; Madison, T. Roosevelt, and Truman as Near-Great; Grant, Harding, and Nixon as the irredeemingly Worst.

Any surprises there? Not if you go over the makeup of the jury. What you'll find is the usual clutch of closed-circuit academics—Arthur Schlesinger Jr., James MacGregor Burns, et al.—whose names regularly appear in full-page *New York Times* ads touting whatever cause du jour People for the American Way is flogging.

Winston Churchill famously predicted that history would treat him well for the good-and-simple reason that "I shall write the history." Lucky for Winnie he wasn't an American leader sailing under the Conservative flag; otherwise all the history he wrote would be buried under Liberal screed in the outer reaches of Ivy League libraries.

Check the record. With few exceptions, America's "unbiased" historians give the same Liberal spin to their subject matter that America's "unbiased" news media give to current events—beginning with their arrantly slanted *Judgment of History*.

It was Schlesinger's father, Arthur Sr., who introduced Oscar Awards–thinking into history studies back in 1962. Like most Liberal historians at the time, Arthur Sr. was in a revisionist state of mind. Though John F. Kennedy had narrowly slipped into the presidency two years earlier, public opinion polls said the American people retained fond memories of his predecessor, Dwight D. Eisenhower.

For the ultra-Liberal Schlesingers this was too much. After twenty years of Democratic rule under Franklin Roosevelt and Harry Truman, they saw Ike's two terms in the White House as an aberration, a passing stumble on America's inexorable march leftward into a golden age of Liberal hegemony. By the 1960s the Republican Party was supposed to be marginalized with non-Keynesian economics in full retreat.

Yet there were those stubborn Gallup numbers telling them that if Eisenhower had been able to run for a third term he'd have been reelected, Jack Kennedy or no Jack Kennedy. Eight years of pounding and ridicule at the hands of Liberal editorialists and supercilious Leftwing commentators hadn't diminished the General's stature one bit.

Baffling. Obviously something had to be done about it: a Judgment of History that would set things right. Just because today's generation of Americans was lost to the Liberal truth about Dwight Eisenhower didn't mean tomorrow's had to be.

It so happened—by no means coincidentally—that at the time Arthur Sr. was busy handing down his stacked Judgment, his son was padding around the Kennedy White House as a mandarin speechwriter.*

---

*Kennedy, like his Harvard-bred predecessor Franklin D. Roosevelt, was shrewd enough to recognize that cultivating influential academics was every bit as important to a sitting president's reputation as cultivating the White House press corps. Could Republican presidents fare better in the Judgment of History by doing the same? Possibly. But by-and-large White House Republicans, though sophisticated in media relations, have been tone-deaf to vibrations from the academic world. Consider Nancy Reagan's choice of the supercilious closet Liberal Edmund Morris as her husband's biographer.

Though Kennedy himself hadn't been in office long enough to be ranked, he was given an advance copy of the list and asked for his thoughts.

JFK, as independent historian Thomas Fleming tells us, was "wryly amused" that Dwight Eisenhower "was near the bottom of the 'average' list," but also "shocked that the poll gave such a high rating to Woodrow Wilson [who] had made a botch of his Mexican intervention in 1914, edged the United States into World War I for 'narrow legalistic reasons' and catastrophically messed up the fight for the Treaty of Versailles and the League of Nations."

That, Kennedy told the Schlesingers, was not the record of a "great" president. But JFK, though usually perceptive about such matters, had in this case missed the point: the Schlesingers' intention wasn't simply to relegate Eisenhower to the ash heap of presidential history but to do Liberal justice to two twentieth century Democratic presidents—Wilson and Harry Truman—whose reputations had suffered at the hands of a benighted American electorate brainwashed by Rightwing propaganda.

Different as their backgrounds were—Wilson the aloof pedagogue, Truman the earthy, machine-spawned politician—the two men shared the fate of all leaders who raise popular hopes and don't deliver as promised: Both left the White House as bitter, rejected men, their presidencies considered abysmal failures.

In Wilson's case, the rejection extended to his intellectual supporters, especially those of civil-libertarian bent. Liberals who today think of Attorney General John Ashcroft as the second coming of Cotton Mather might (though they undoubtedly won't) read up on the history of Wilson's Justice Department, where wartime Attorney General A. Mitchell Palmer carried out—in the words of Liberal columnist Walter Lippmann—"a reign of terror in which honest thought is impossible."

Thirty years later, the same Walter Lippmann, by then dean of the Liberal Media Establishment, was bemoaning the future of the Republic under the leadership of Harry Truman—an accidental president, the columnist told his readers, who wasn't fit, by either intellect or temperament, to sit in the chair once occupied by Franklin Delano Roosevelt.

Not that Truman's widespread unpopularity—by the end of his term his Gallup numbers were running in the low twenties—was due solely to his having worked in Roosevelt's long shadow. For the most part, he did it on his own, transmogrifying over the years from the humble vice president who succeeded FDR in 1945 into a short-fused petty politician who loaded his White House staff with influence-peddling cronies; had to be restrained by court order from imperially seizing the nation's steel mills; engaged in acrimonious feuds with anyone who crossed him (the Marine Corps, charged a peevish Truman, "has a propaganda machine bigger than Stalin's."); and capped a stormy half-decade as commander-in-chief by involving the country in a bloody "limited" war in Korea whose inconclusive result we still pay the price for half-a-century later.

No matter. By the time the Liberal revisionists had cosmetized the record, all that remained was the myth of Saint Woodrow and the legend of Give-'em-Hell-Harry: Wilson, the Liberal idealist martyred by a willful band of small-minded Republican obstructionists in the United States Senate; Truman, the plainspoken underdog who, in the autumn of 1948, fought and won the Good Fight against the dark forces of Reaction.

Have the cosmetics stood the test of time? Judge for yourself: In the autumn of 1976, a Republican president behind in the polls cheerfully threw himself into the role of Harry Truman, an underdog running against the odds. (That Jerry Ford's strategy didn't succeed might have been due to the fact that, unlike his hero Harry, he had no stomach for calling his opponent a "front man for the same clique who backed Hitler, Mussolini, and Tojo.")

But more: A quarter-century later, Conservative editorial writers who support George W. Bush's vision for the Middle East could pay this Republican president no greater compliment than to say he was acting . . . *Wilsonian!*

Hmmm . . . It's enough to make a cynic think that maybe the old Sage of Dearborn was right after all. The Judgment of History, said old Henry Ford as he approached the end of his days, "is bunk."

K

Katherine and Karl. Bonnie and Clyde in the Great Florida Heist of 2000.

Kennedys. The First Family of Liberaldom in forty-nine states and the District of Columbia.

Kerrymandering. (1) Liberwock confabulation, northeast United States, *viz.* the articulation, within the space of a single fifteen-minute time-frame, of two or more conflicting positions on the same issue; (2) Legislative Seinfeldism.

NOTHING DOING

"It's a show about nothing."

> —JERRY SEINFELD ON BEING ASKED TO EXPLAIN THE ABSENCE OF ANY THEME TO HIS LONG-RUNNING TELEVISION SERIES.

"Sometimes your accomplishments are not in what you get done but in what you stop other people from doing."

> —JOHN KERRY ON BEING ASKED TO EXPLAIN THE ABSENCE OF ANY LEGISLATION TO PROVE HE SPENT NINETEEN YEARS IN THE UNITED STATES SENATE.

kids. Term of endearment once applied only to pre-kindergarten children who believe in Santa Claus and the Tooth Fairy; now applied, post–Chicago '68, to college-age rioters who believe in Che and Mao.

OUR KIDS OUT THERE

When the anti-Vietnam War demonstrators at the 1968 Democratic convention turned violent, the Chicago police responded in kind, dispersing the "Yippie" mob with tear gas and billyclubs. On one side were the campus-radical offspring of affluent families; on the other, the Chicago police, blue-collar offspring of working-class families. Reporting on the scene, New York Times columnist Tom Wicker, his sympathies for the rioters showing, deplored the horror of it all with the unctuous line, "Those were our kids out there"; to which the answer came in the form of a bellow from an earthbound Chicago alderman: "What about the cops? They're our kids, too."

Kissinger, a.k.a. **Dr. Strangelove.** Cambridge River don turned Nixonite, reviled in Harvard Yard as a Traitor to his Class.

L

leave no child behind. Politically uplifting slogan for a federally-funded educational program jointly sponsored by the Bush White House and Senator Ted Kennedy. Not to be confused with a school-board advisory to absent-minded bus drivers in East Passaic, New Jersey.

legislative liaison. As described by the mainstream media, Democratic public affairs counselors on Capitol Hill who represent private sector interests, never to be mistaken for . . .

lobbyists. As described by the mainstream media, Republican influence-peddlers on Capitol Hill working for corporate fat cats.

"lying crooks". Republicans, as described by moderate presidential candidate John Kerry, reflecting his oft-expressed desire to stick to the issues.

TRULY STUPID LIBERAL IDEAS

Allowing lawyers to advertise, a.k.a. **legalized ambulance chasing.** Old enough to remember when people referred to the practice of law as a "profession"? Those licensed to practice, it was said, were "officers of the court," dedicated to the pursuit of justice, not profit. True, the high standard didn't always hold, but at least there *was* a standard, something more than we find at the bar of justice since the Liberwocked American Bar Association sanctioned consumer advertising in the unhinged seventies. (See ad on following page.)

M

mainstream. Wherever Tom Daschle happens to be up the creek at a given moment in history.

mainstream media. To Liberal tastes, any segment of the media that reports the news in a politically correct manner. For instance, imagine the present-day *Washington Post* covering a controversial Republican president's address in a small Pennsylvania village, circa 1863:

ABE LAYS EGG AT GETTYSBURG

GETTYSBURG, PA—Nov. 19—President Lincoln, in what White House aides billed as a "nonpolitical" speech, dedicated a military cemetery here today before a sparse, unresponsive crowd estimated by local authorities at fewer than 300 people.

In a tactical move clearly designed to get the political jump on Gen. George B. McClellan, his probable Democratic opponent, Mr. Lincoln made one of his rare trips outside Washington to visit this vote-rich Keystone State. Judging by early reaction to his appearance, however, the White House strategy appears to have backfired.

Not only was the president's address sharply criticized by political experts for being too brief, but he was upstaged by the main speaker of the day, the brilliant public orator Everett Hale. Moreover, Mr. Lincoln's glaring failure to mention McClellan or Gen. George G. Meade, the victorious Union commander of the battle fought here in July, casts doubt on White House staff claims that the trip was "purely nonpolitical."

One veteran political observer, noting recent charges that the Lincoln administration has created a "credibility gap" between itself and the public, termed the president's omission of McClellan's and Meade's names from his speech text "a serious blunder that will come back to haunt him in next year's election."

"This is another example of the sloppy White House staff work that has plagued the administration since the day Lincoln took office," commented another observer on receiving news that the president's speech had been hurriedly scribbled on the back of an envelope en route to the speech site.

Mr. Lincoln delivered his remarks in the same high-pitched, irritating Middle Western nasal inflection that characterized his past public addresses. Another criticism was that the speech, in the words of one Gettysburg resident, "didn't say anything we haven't already heard."

"My family and I came out to see and listen to the president of the United States, and all we got was a puny two minutes," said another disenchanted localite.

Mr. Lincoln remained unsmiling throughout his visit to this small eastern Pennsylvania village. Aides claimed the president's solemn demeanor was simply "appropriate to the occasion," but knowledgeable Washington sources have indicated that serious problems in Mr. Lincoln's home life more likely account for his grim public visage in recent months.

In support of this view, it was noted that Mrs. Lincoln did not accompany the president here.

The president, who has not held a major news conference in two years, refused reporters' requests that he answer questions following his address. In the speech itself, Mr. Lincoln said that the men who died in the battle here gave their lives in order "that this nation, under God, shall have a new birth of freedom—and that government of the people, by the people, for the people, shall not perish from the earth."

However the president, who was elected three years ago on a pledge to preserve the Union, again failed to provide details on any fresh administration initiative to achieve this objective.

# # #

mandate. Elusive goal of every Republican president, even those like Ronald Reagan who carry forty-nine states.

WHO'S GOT THE MANDATE?

IT IS AXIOMATIC AMONG LIBERALS THAT NO Republican president, with the possible exception of Abraham Lincoln, has ever had a legitimate claim to the office. Not that any have suspended the Constitution and seized the White House by military coup*; only that the very premise of the Liberal faith— that they alone hold the key to the people's hopes and

---

*Though as Susan Sontag and Barbra Streisand frequently warn, there is always that possibility.

aspirations—precludes the possibility that a majority of American voters, unless duped or drugged, would ever willingly vote against their interests. From this it follows that the only reasonable explanation for Republican victories in the past half-century lies not in the American people delivering a mandate but in . . .

- Eisenhower blinding voters with a vapid smile and slick Madison Avenue techniques in the 1950s
- Nixon winning with Dirty Tricks in 1968 and '72
- Reagan using cue-cards and an October Surprise in 1980
- Bush the Elder going racist with the Willie Horton TV spot in 1988
- Bush the Younger, like Ponce de Leon, simply stealing Florida in 2000

manicured lawns. Liberal media metaphor for lily-white suburban neighborhoods inhabited by bourgeois Starbucks customers insensitive to the plight of those dispossessed in a soulless society of bottom-line corporate values. Note other liberal metaphors for free-market American culture (e.g., Formica tabletops, plastic anything).

TRuly StuPid LiBeRAL idEAS

The Mandatory Auto Helmet Act of 2008.
No, we're not there yet but given current
trends, Big Nanny, i.e., the Department of Trans-
portation, will see to it that states will soon pass
laws requiring not only motorcyclists but also
drivers and passengers in cars and trucks to
adorn their heads with plastic as they travel
down streets with warning signs that read . . .

SMOKE-FREE NEIGHBORHOOD

TOBACCO USERS WILL BE PROSECUTED

. . . to get to restaurants operating under caloric
guidelines furnished by the Federal Bureau of
Obesity Control (FBOC).

McCarthyism! Circa 1950-55, to accuse someone of
being a Communist. More recently, to accuse a Liberal of
something for which he has no defense.

meaningful dialogue. (1) Any exchange of views between Liberals and Others in which the Liberal does at least three-fourths of the talking and Others agree; (2) Two or more Liberal monologues taking place simultaneously.

meaningful negotiations. We got our way.

mean-spirited. Gratuitous, below-the-belt gibes designed to defame or otherwise hurt a public figure (e.g., Rush Limbaugh's repeated references to Chappaquiddick and Monica Lewinsky). Not to be confused with **free-spirited** (e.g., National Public Radio's Nina Totenberg's devout wish that Senator Jesse Helms "get AIDS from a transfusion or that one of his grandchildren will get it").

Military-Industrial Complex. (1) The foremost threat to world peace, along with the Pentagon, Joint Chiefs of Staff, National Security Council, CIA, and Richard Perle on steroids. (2) In former days, when FDR was commander-in-chief and the enemy was Hitler's Germany, what is now called the Military-Industrial menace was affectionately known as the Arsenal of Democracy. See also former president Jimmy Carter's delineative take on arms reduction, *Why Can't We All Just Get Along?* (Pangloss Press).

moderate Republican. A Republican who, if he or she were on trial for being a Republican, would be acquitted for lack of evidence.

LIBOQUERY

Dear Doctor Libuthnot: I've heard the term "moderate Republican" applied to politicians, but never "moderate Democrat." Why not?

—CONFUSED READER

Dear Confused Reader: Good question. The press never uses the term "moderate Democrat," presumably because by Liberal lights all Democrats are moderate. Unless of course they occasionally vote with Republicans—in which case they're called "conservative" Democrats (e.g., Georgia Senator Zell Miller).

N

Naderites, a.k.a. **the Greens.** Far-Left Liberal sect occasionally centered around the person of political gadfly Ralph Nader, a self-made man who worships his creator.

Neanderthal Conservatives. Warhawk wing of the Republican Party that wanted to "lob a nuke into the mens' room of the Kremlin" (Barry Goldwater, 1964), since supplanted by **Neo-Conservatives,** warhawk wing of the Republican Party that merely wants to lob a nuke into the mens' room of the Palais Elysée.

Negative campaigning. Dirty semantic tricks practiced by Rightwing hit men, as when a presidential candidate with a 100 percent Americans for Democratic Action rating is described as "Liberal." See also **Progressive.**

nonconformist. By Liberal standards, one at odds with the stifling standards and mores of bourgeois, suburb-dwelling Middle American society, i.e., one who conforms to Liberal standards and mores.

nonpartisan. Liberal Democrats in mugwump drag (e.g., the League of Women Voters, Brookings Institution, any organization that employs the terms **relevant, viable,** and/or **responsive** in its nonpolitical mission statement).

NPR. National Public Radio. Drive-time ear candy for the Prius and white wine set. See also **PBS.**

ON THIS DATE IN LIBERWOCK HISTORY

May 7, 1962: James Earl Carter listed himself on the Georgia Democratic primary ballot as "Jimmy" and was elected to the state senate on a promise that he had no further political ambitions and would run for no other office.

O

obscene. Liberal pejorative applied to "outrageous" corporate profits; not, however, applicable to pornographic magazines or motion pictures.

TRᴜʟʏ Sᴛᴜᴘɪᴅ Lɪʙᴇʀᴀʟ ɪᴅEAS

Renaming the White House. The wonder is that an effort wasn't made to do this during the Clinton years. But brace for it, along about the time the next Liberwock president (having tested the waters by re-naming Lee Highway and Custer National Forest) goes for broke on the Sensitivity Issue.

New York Times headline, circa July 2012:

. . . .

OPRAH CALL-IN TO DECIDE NEW "WHITE HOUSE" NAME

. . . .

Oprah! The must-do stop for Liberal candidates in pursuit of the touchy-feely vote; under no circumstances to be confused by campaign schedulers with the . . .

O'Reilly Factor, which, second only to AK-47 gun shows sponsored by the National Rifle Association, is No-Man's Land for politicians of touchy-feely persuasion.

outreach. Belated pandering to minority voter blocs overlooked in past elections. Note also **inclusion.**

outsourcing. During the Clinton years, the far-sighted exportation of American economic resources to friendly peoples, the better to capture the hearts and minds of the global work force; during the Bush years, abandoning American labor to enhance the profits of ruthless multinational corporations.

overreact. Any reaction whatsoever to problems toward which Liberals do not wish action to be taken. Note sister term **counterproductive.**

P

panacea. Non-Liberal solution; as distinguished from **solution:** Liberal panacea.

patriotism. A virulent form of **ethnocentrism** chiefly characterized by belligerent flag-waving and demands for excessive funding of the Military-Industrial Complex. Note also **jingoism, chauvinism,** and **superpatriotism**—as in Professor Noah Chomsky's classic, *Valley Forge and the Superpatriotic Excrescence in American Life.*

PBS. Public Broadcasting System. Eye candy for the tofu and British broadcasting set.

peace process, a.k.a. **Oslo Accords.** A process going nowhere replaced by a Road Map showing the way.

A MASSACHUSETTS LIBERAL
IN THE CONTINENTAL CONGRESS

Continental Congress of the United Colonies
Independence Hall
Philadelphia, Pennsylvania

January 14, 1777

To the Honorable George Washington, Esq.
General in Command
The Continental Army
Somewhere in New Jersey

My Deare General,

Yours of January 3d having been received, I take
this Opportunity to Inform You that said Request
for Additional Funds to conduct the Operations
you propose has been Duly Considered and
Rejected by the Committee on Finance. Following,
for Your Edification and Enlightenment, are the
Various and Sundry Reasons for said Rejection:

I

Should You have any Doubt that Your Reckless
Christmas Venture across the Delaware was anything but an Unmitigated Diplomatic Blunder, I

enclose Herewith a Letter of Protest from the Landgraf of Hesse-Cassel pointing out that the Hessian Subjects assaulted in the City of Trenton that night comprised a visiting Conclave of Archaeologists rather than the Mercenary Army reported by your Faulty Intelligence Service. Needless to add, we have Duly Apologized for your ill-advised Act of Aggression, but nevertheless Find Ourselves committed to the Payment of Reparations not only to the Aggrieved Landgraf but the Friedrich Wilhelm Society of Central European Archaeologists.

II

Reports continue to arrive regarding the Contemptible Disregard of Soldiers under Your Command for the Care and Nurture of the Environment, particularly the Egregious Toll by Random Foragers on the Quail population (*Quaccular Galliformes*) indigenous to the Region; which species, let me Remind, has been placed on the Highly Endangered List under terms of the International Compact on Nature Conservancy; not to mention Complaints received from sundry Allergy-Challenged Villagers in eastern Pennsylvania regarding the Deleterious Effects of Second-

Hand Smoke caused by the Indiscriminate Use of Tobacco Products by Members of your Army.

III

Finally, there is the Matter of the ongoing Embedment in your Ranks of the Extremist Pamphleteer Tom Paine, whose most recent Screed, *The Crisis,* can only Exacerbate Tensions at a time when, thanks to the Good Offices of General Arnold, a Window of Opportunity has opened for Meaningful Negotiations leading toward a Rapprochement and Healing Process with His Majesty's Government.

IV

In any Case, we are out of Money. What little we had has been Expended on Implementation of a University of Pennsylvania Study of the Infra-Structural Needs of the City of Philadelphia.

Yr. Obdt Servant,
Y. A. Liberthwaite

People for the American Way (PAW). Liberal public interest organization founded by Norman Lear, not to be confused with the **American Conservative Union (ACU)**, Rightwing special interest organization founded by Torquemada circa 1495. PAW favors God, Motherhood, and Apple Pie—to the extent that God stays out of public schools, Motherhood is defined as embracing male as well as female couples, and Apple Pie is made only with organically-grown fruit. For information about other Liberal public interest groups, visit http://www.BillClintonforMount Rushmore.org and the George oro Institute for Campaign Finance Reform.

people of color. Another turn on the wheel of Liberally Correct euphemisms used to describe members of the Non-Caucasian underclass. For colorizing reference to members of the Caucasian underclass, see **redneck.**

people's right to know, whether they want to or not—e.g., Bill Clinton's preference in shorts; what Carmen Electra has for breakfast; the unabridged doctor's report (with diagrams) of the president's latest colonoscopy; and the number, disposition, and firearm capability of White House security forces. (For an example of media indisposition when denied full disclosure, see box on facing page.)

politicize. To unsportingly direct the people's attention to an issue involving the people's interests. Note also **rise above politics,** which Republican members of Congress are said to do when they break party ranks (e.g., Vermont Senator James Jeffords) as distinguished from **selling out,** which Democratic members of Congress are said to do whenever they break party ranks (e.g., Georgia Senator Zell Miller).

Pragmatic Approach to Problems (PAP). Liberal approach that works. If it doesn't, blame Rightwing underfunding, call the situation problematic, and **move on.**

POLITICS ANYONE?

> "Whenever I hear somebody say he wants to take something out of politics, I know what he means is take it out of my politics and put it into his politics."
>
> —ALABAMA GOVERNOR BIG JIM FOLSOM, CIRCA 1955.

premises and priorities. Liberal first-things-first, as expressed by Arthur Schlesinger Jr.'s dictum, "We must reorder the premises and priorities of our society," i.e., *do it my way.* For definitive work on what happens when you don't reorder your priorities, see Al Gore's *How I Reinvented Government (But Lost Tennessee).*

progressive. A Liberal with presidential ambitions.

WHEN IS A LIBERAL . . .?

IT WAS ARIZONA CONGRESSMAN MORRIS Udall who first signaled the end of the Great Society era when he announced he would run for the 1976 Democratic presidential nomination as a Progressive, not a Liberal.

Why? A rare Liberal with a self-deprecating sense of humor, Udall was his own candid self when he told reporters that, like the storied dog food that "dogs just don't like," the term Liberal for some reason turned people off. Only loyalty to his old party leader kept Udall from explaining the turnoff as a massive backlash against Lyndon Johnson's Great Society programs.

Like Britain's Liberal Party in the early years of the twentieth century, American Liberals finally got their way in the 1960s, pushing all their panacean programs through with a vengeance. History repeats: Within a matter of years, British Liberals interested in political survival were calling themselves *Laborites*. By the mid-1970s, their American soulmates were following suit, running for semantic cover.

Udall was forthright in changing his label in 1976,

but in typical fashion the Liberal who won the Democratic nomination that year slipslid the issue: "I don't like to categorize," Jimmy Carter told an inquiring reporter in New Hampshire. *"I don't see myself as a Liberal or Conservative or the like."*

No matter. Whatever semantic rock Liberal politicians choose to hide under, there's no mistaking the fact that with few exceptions—e.g., the late Paul Wellstone, the spaced Dennis Kucinich—Leftwing politicians over the past quarter-century have been in denial about their Liberalism.

So too, though for different motives, their L——— friends in the media. The worst-kept secret along the Eastern Media Belt (other than the identity of Al Franken's toupee-maker) is that eight out of ten reporters, editors, correspondents, and columnists working the national political scene breathe, eat, and vote Liberal. Yet, like the greatest slipslider of them all, they persist in claiming they *have not had sex with that woman.**

---

*So reluctant are political writers and commentators to confess their Liberalism that Fox cable news had a hard time filling the Liberal slot on one of its most popular primetime talk shows. The original concept—to get James Carville to go head-to-head with Sean Hannity every weeknight—fell through when Carville insisted on top billing, i.e., *Carville & Hannity.* Flummoxed, the show's producers had to call Central Casting to fill the role; which is to say, Alan Colmes is not really a Liberal. He's an actor hired to play the part of one with, as one producer put it, "as much conviction as he can possibly muster."

Consider the case of Walter Cronkite, caught *in flagrante* every weeknight through three decades of anchoring the CBS *Evening News*. Only after Cronkite retired did he reveal, full-blown, that *Yes, yes, yes, I'm a Liberal and proud of it!*

Out of the closet. And Dan Rather, Cronkite's successor who insists, despite years of cloying interviews with Hillary Clinton, that he's a political neuter? Rather's a face-lifted seventy-two now, due for retirement in a few years. Can we expect a Liberal-outing from him? Possibly. But, as Dan himself would say, don't bet your last heifer on it.

Q

quotas. Politically incorrect affirmative action.

TRULY STUPID LIBERAL IDEAS

Hawaii Apology Resolution, passed by Congress and signed by President William J. Clinton, November 23, 1993. It was one of the paradigmatic highlights of Bill Clinton's first year in office, a self-reproaching, all-hankies-out expression of remorse . . . Or is it possible you haven't heard of it? If not, look it up in the Congressional Record of October 27 and November 15, 1993. Or check it out at http://www.hawaii-nation.org/. Here's what you'll find, U.S. Public Law 103-150 (an excerpt):

Whereas, the indigenous Hawaiian people never directly relinquished their claims to their inherent sovereignty as a people or over their national lands to the United States, either through their monarch or through a plebiscite or referendum; and . . .

Whereas, the Native Hawaiian people are determined to preserve, develop, and transmit to future generation their ancestral territory,

*and their cultural identity in accordance with
their own spiritual and traditional beliefs,
customs, practices, language, and social
institutions;*

*Now, Therefore be it Resolved, THE CON-
GRESS apologizes to Native Hawaiians on
behalf of the people of the United States for
the overthrow of the Kingdom of Hawaii . . .
and the deprivation of the rights of Native
Hawaiians to self-determination;*

*expresses its commitment to acknowledge
the ramifications of the overthrow of the
Kingdom of Hawaii, in order to provide a
proper foundation for reconciliation between
the United States and the Native Hawaiian
people . . .*

Clear enough? If not, it's because, as
Hawaiian Senator Daniel Akaka argued in support of his Resolution, "Few Americans know
that the Kingdom of Hawaii was a highly or-
ganized, civilized, and sovereign nation . . . . "
Until, that is, the Mainland Barbarians turned
the pristine islands into a vulgar tourist trap
and provoked the peace-loving Japanese into
bombing Oahu.

But that's another story. Maybe even the trigger for another Resolution of Apology in the years ahead ...

Whereas the indigenous Hawaiian people, having no quarrel with the Government or people of Japan, never directly agreed to the establishment of a U.S. Naval Base at Pearl Harbor ...

Never happen? Don't be too sure. In the decade since Bill Clinton giddily signed Akaka's Apology Resolution, not only has the "healing" not occurred but militants in Hawaii have launched an all-out movement for independence and sovereignty. Good news for Akaka? Not necessarily. If Hawaii secedes from the Union, he'll lose his job as senator.

On the other hand, he might, all Apologies considered, end up with a promotion: An independent sovereign Hawaii would need, in addition to more-and-better Apologies, a king! Would you believe . . . His Royal Highness Daniel the First?

R

racist. Any corporate CEO who doesn't make a six-figure contribution to Jesse Jackson's Rainbow Coalition during the Reverend's annual Wall Street shakedown tour.

reform, a.k.a. **campaign finance reform.** As viewed by independently wealthy Liberals (e.g., Jay Rockefeller, Jon Corzine), legislation designed to keep the corruptive influence of other people's money out of politics.

regulations, a.k.a. **The Federal Register.** Liberal Scripture, Old Testament (FDR) and New (JFK).

DEAR VIRGINIA

(IN WHICH A LIBERWOCK EDITOR TAKES UP THE SANTA CLAUS QUESTION IN 2004)

Letter to the Editor of the *New York Sun*, November 1897:

I am 8 years old. Some of my little friends say there is no Santa Claus. Papa says, "If you see it in The Sun, it's so." Please tell me the truth, is there a Santa Claus?

Sincerely, Virginia O'Hanlon

More than a century later *Sun* editor Francis P. Church's reply to young Virginia O'Hanlon remains a classic American Christmas story.

"Yes, Virginia," wrote Church in one of the most famous holiday editorials ever published, "there is a Santa Claus. He exists as certainly as love and generosity and devotion abound and give to your life its highest beauty and joy. Alas! how dreary would be the world if there were no Santa Claus!"

Lucky little girl. She lived in a time when an eight-year-old newspaper reader could write the editor of a major New York daily and get back a straight answer.

But suppose little Virginia had written her letter not at the end of the nineteenth but at the beginning of the twenty-first century? And not to the *Sun*, which has long since folded, but to the leading New York daily of the day?

Unlucky little girl. She'd probably get back an e-mail that read something like this:

. . . . , , , , , ...

FROM: Bill Keller
<bkeller@NewYorkTimes.com>

DATE: 2004/09/25 Sat PM 0409 EST
TO: MsVirginiaOHanlon@verizon.net

Dear Ms. O'Hanlon: Your query regarding the existence of the avuncular holiday personage known as Santa Claus has been received and forwarded to appropriate Departments for their investigation and input. To date we have ascertained the following:

A perambulatory entrepreneur of that description is indeed known to the Department of Commerce, Immigration and Naturalization Service, and Securities and Exchange Commission. But neither he nor his enterprise, a multi-national entity known as "North Pole Toy & Amusement, Inc.," are officially registered with any of said agencies, in flagrant violation of numerous sections of the U.S. Code.

In addition, usually reliable sources at the Federal Aviation Authority inform us that no fewer than 267 warrants alleging unauthorized deviation from flight plans (North Pole to United States) are outstanding against one "S. Claus, a.k.a. St. Nicholas, a.k.a. Father Christmas" for the period 1977-2003, over and above 412 pending charges of traversing international air space without a license.

Nor, Ms. O'Hanlon, is that all. Similar

charges have been filed against the Chairman/CEO of North Pole Toy & Amusement, Inc. by (a) the National Labor Relations Board (failure to meet minimum wage standards for documented though non-unionized elves); (b) the Consumer Products Safety Commission (failure to apply bilingual warning labels to children's toys); (c) the Food and Drug Administration (failure to provide nutritional data on lactose, glucose, fructose, and other carbohydrate stocking-stuffers); not to mention a request for injunctive relief filed in the Ninth Federal Circuit Court (San Francisco) by the Environmental Protection Agency for—I quote directly from the brief—"your reckless overwork, despite recurrent warnings, of a select herd of flying Rangifer tarandas, a species second only to the Percina tanasi of the Tennessee River on our Agency's Endangered list."

I could, if space permitted, go on at some length. But suffice it to say that your question is both relevant and timely, the bottom-line being that Yes, Virginia, there is indeed a Santa Claus, but rest well, for your government is hot on his trail.

relativity. Liberal absolute.

reparations. Punitive damages paid to people other than those damaged by people other than those who did the damage. See also **Al Sharpton's annuity.**

TRULY STUPID LIBERAL IDEAS

Voting rights for felons. As comedian Steve Allen once put it, "You can't write satire these days because the real thing shows up every morning in the news," e.g., a campaign on the part of the looney-tune Left to enfranchise killers, rapists, robbers, embezzlers . . .

VIDEOTAPE, "SNOPES FOR GOVERNOR"

TV spot (60 sec.)/
Target audience: California state prison inmates—
(For airing halftime, Oakland Raiders-Pittsburgh
Steelers game 10/17/07)

VIDEO	AUDIO
LOU BASHEM, an Armani-suited male on Rodeo Drive, L.A.	BACKGROUND MUSIC (sotto) Johnny Cash's "Folsom Prison Blues," then BASHEM: "Stuck in Folsom Prison?" So was I this time last year but that's another story . . . Hello, I'm Lou Bashem, a.k.a. "Quickhand Louie," and I'm here to tell you about your friend and mine, Clem Snopes— the only candidate runnin' for Governor this year who cares about us cons and ex-cons. Fed up with poundin'

A MERCEDES 560 driven by a SWIMSUIT MODEL drives up, parks behind Bashem.

(Flashing "V" sign)

The SWIMSUIT MODEL gets out of car, joins Bashem. She's wearing a sash—SNOPES FOR GOVERNOR

rocks? Hard-ass guards who cut off your conjugal? Turn-downs when you're up for parole? Here's your chance to do somethin' about it. Your vote for Clem Snopes for Governor is gonna bring in catered chow, compassionate wardens, and a feel-your-pain parole board that won't say "No." Vote Snopes for Governor, and who knows? This time next year, you could be here in L.A., a chick on one arm, a Rolex on the other—Ain't that right, Candy?

MODEL: (bussing him) Whatever you say, Big Boy . . .

VOICE-OVER: On Four November vote early, vote often, and make your vote Snopes for Governor. The preceding paid for by the Greater California League for Compassionate Stir Time, Arianna Huffington, Chairperson.

responsibility. Pre-modern ecclesiastical term *re* individual free will, co-opted circa 1960 by the liberal construct . . .

root cause, which places ultimate responsibility where it properly belongs, on (1) a regressive socio-economic system, (2) a heartrending childhood of deprivation and abuse, and/or (3) a psychosomatic problem beyond the individual's control.

LAYwERWoCKY

"He suffers from a molecular imbalance exacerbated by stress."

—LIBERWOCK ATTORNEY REPRESENTING A COLLEGE PRESIDENT IN THE NATION'S CAPITAL CHARGED WITH MAKING OBSCENE PHONE CALLS TO A POLICE OFFICER'S WIFE.

S

scary. MTV-derived term used by Liberals to dramatize their distress over the possibility of a Conservative being elected (or reelected) to the presidency. For instance, in 1968 columnist Jimmy Breslin took an oath to leave the country after Richard Nixon's victory over Hubert Humphrey; in the year 2000, the actor Alec Baldwin said he'd take the next plane to Europe if George W. Bush became president. Neither, at last report, has left his barstool.

See-and-Say (a.k.a. "Whole-Word") Method of Reading Instruction. The systum used by all enlitened educashunalists to teech our kids how to decifer thoz stranj things called words that com off the Internet (as opposed to the bakward systum called Fonics that warped the minds of past generashuns of American students), and if you think this is bad riting you shood see whut passes for spelling at Harvard, Yale, and Cal-Berkeley these daze.

self-esteem. That which an atavistic society denies its young and impressionable through the encouragement of games that stress the competitive rather than holistic nature of life on Planet Earth.

BASEBALL, LIBERWOCK STYLE

ABSOLUTE JUDGMENTS (E.G., BALLS-AND- strikes, hits-and-runs, fair balls-and-foul, errors-and-outs) are prohibited, allowing each player an opportunity to do his own beatific thing.

All authority symbols are eliminated (though not, needless to say, in terms of the traditional outcry that woefully bespeaks the violent strain coursing through American culture, i.e., "*Kill the umpire!*")

Teams are run not by arbitrary managers/coaches but by player council decision, the better to provide players a participatory voice in those inning-by-inning decisions that affect their welfare.

Concerned-and-committed fans are encouraged to adopt a pluralistic rather than monolithic attitude toward players, the outmoded concept of "home team" no longer being applicable to a sports world-in-ferment.

For an extended discussion of this last point, see Jonathan Schell's *One Team or None!* (Afflatus Press).

sexist, a.k.a. **male chauvinist.** As defined by the Grand Sanhedrin of Feminism (Germaine Greer, Gloria Steinem, Rosie O'Donnell), anyone to the Androgen Right of Alan Alda.

Solid South. Benign Democratic hold on white, Confederate-flag-waving Southern voters, 1870-1960, not to be compared with . . .

Southern Strategy. Malign Republican campaign to convert white Confederate-flag-waving Democratic voters, 1968-2004. (See Appendix 4, **Six Liberal Myths.**)

spin. That which conservative White House spokesmen do when interpreting the news; not to be confused with **interpretive reporting,** that which Liberal journalists do when spinning the news.

stereotype. In Liberal eyes, calumnious generalizations about minority groups perpetuated by ignorant white Southern rednecks and bigoted Christian fundamentalists.

ON THIS DATE IN LIBERWOCK HISTORY

March 10, 1955: Young Bill Clinton first uttered the phrase "I feel your pain" to a pig-tailed nine-year-old classmate just returned from the dentist's office.

T

talk radio, a.k.a. **the Chattering Masses** (as opposed to the Chattering Classes, e.g., Jennings, Brokaw, Rather, et al.). Proof positive that Marconi must have been part of the Vast Rightwing Conspiracy.

task force. Liberal administration's modus operandi in dealing with complex problems. For intractable problems, try a **commission.**

tax, spend, and elect, a.k.a. **Hopkins's Choice.** Liberal formula for perpetual governance first advanced by presidential advisor Harry Hopkins during Franklin D. Roosevelt's first term. For another view however, see election returns, 1994-2002.

"Tell it like it is". Translated from the Liberwock, "Tell it my way." See also **meaningful dialogue.**

thrust. In Liberal parlance, that which is being meaningfully articulated, e.g., "The thrust of former Gov. Dean's remarks was that his previous remarks were not only taken out of context but those that were reported accurately had been misconstrued as meaning he was in favor of extending Medicare to veterinary hospitals, when in fact . . . "

TRuly StuPid LiBeral idEAS

Putting women into frontline combat. All in the name of equal rights, equal opportunity. Proving that the Liberwock virus, far from being restricted to Ivy League campuses and Eastern Seaboard editorial rooms, thrives even in Donald Rumsfeld's Pentagon.

U

uncivil union. The International Brotherhood of Teamsters (particularly when supporting Republican candidates).

unacceptable! Said by family members to be the first word uttered by Liberwock Congressman Henry Waxman (D–Calif.) shortly after birth. See also **woefully inadequate.**

undocumented. Liberwock for illegal, as when a shoplifter leaves a Wal-Mart with stolen merchandise and can't produce a sales slip. In Liberal terminology this becomes an **undocumented sale.** See also Liberally incorrect **illegal alien.**

unilateralism. White House commitment to a foreign policy initiative absent prior consultation with Ted Turner.

United Nations. In the eyes of the *New York Times*, the last best hope for peace; in the eyes of the New York Police Department, 86,275,343 unpaid parking tickets.

United States. In metro-Liberal eyes, merely one of the two-hundred-odd members of the United Nations.

up to speed. Dennis Kucinich hitting *Mach 4* on his most recent journey to Pluto.

ON THIS DATE IN LIBERWOCK HISTORY

October 7, 1958: Eighteen-year-old Martin Sheen took part in his first mass demonstration, picketing City Hall to protest the mayor's refusal to declare Dayton, Ohio, a Cold War neutral.

V

Vast Rightwing Conspiracy. (1) Latter-day remnants or descendants of the Know-nothing Party, Knights of the White Camellia, Ku Klux Klan, German-American Bund and John Birch Society, combined in force to thwart the will of the American people; (2) As led astray by Rush Limbaugh, Fox News, and Lee Greenwood's rendition of "God Bless America," the fifty-seven percent of American voters who, through two elections, failed to cast their ballots for Bill Clinton for president. (See now **The Enemies List,** extracted from **Hillary's (Secret) Diary.**)

THE ENEMIES* LIST
(THE WHITE HOUSE YEARS)

SHE DIDN'T CALL IT THAT, OF COURSE, BUT THERE there they were, no fewer than 427 names, written in meticulous script, on the last ten pages of Hillary Clinton's (Secret) Diary. Why the list? In this case HRC's candor gives way to the Clinton White House instinct for cover-up: She tells her diary that it's merely "a compilation for future reference." The question is, future reference for what? Readers can draw their own conclusions, but, in any case, following on the next page are those names—fifty-two in number—set apart from all others by Hillary's special application of distinguishing asterisks.

Roger Ailes*

Fred Barnes*

William Bennett*

Pat Buchanan*

William F. Buckley*

George H.W. Bush*

George W. Bush*

Jeb Bush*

Dick Cheney*

Ann Coulter*

Tom DeLay*

Matt Drudge*

Jerry Falwell*

Gennifer Flowers**

Newt Gingrich*

Lucianne Goldberg**

Rudy Giuliani*

Sean Hannity

Britt Hume*

Henry Hyde*

Cliff Johnson*

Paula Jones**

David Keene*

Charles Krauthammer*

William Kristol

Judge Royce C. Lamberth*

Monica Lewinsky**

Jean Lewis*

Rush Limbaugh*

Dick Morris*

Rupert Murdoch*

Peggy Noonan*

Bob Novak*

Bill O'Reilly*

George Pataki*

Larry Patterson*

Roger Perry*

Wesley Pruden*

Ralph Reed*

Pat Robertson*

William Safire*

Richard Mellen Scaife*

Craig Shirley*

Kenneth Starr*

Barbra Streisand**

Cal Thomas*

Linda Tripp**

R. Emmett Tyrrell*

David Watkins*

George Will*

Kathleen Willey**

vast wasteland. Pertaining to Liberal cultural values (circa 1961), all network television fare, as described by FCC Chairman Newton Minow; circa 2004, everything on prime-time television politically east of *West Wing*.

victory, a.k.a. **"V for ————,"** circa 1941-45. Archaic triumphalist concept, since supplanted by **Negotiated Settlement** (Korea, 1953) and **Strategic Withdrawal** (Vietnam, 1974).

vision. Second only to **meaningful,** the most overused word in the Liberal vocabulary. (For prime example of a visionary gone over-the-top, see below.)

I HAVE A VISION

"We must stand for something more magnificent even than a grand slam home run. We ought to have a Grand Slam Society where all of us have a chance to work together for a better tomorrow."

—BILL CLINTON ON JACKIE ROBINSON,
COMMEMORATION CEREMONY, 1997.

W

W. In states colored red, symbol of winning; in states colored blue, the Mark of the Beast. Note also **"Dubya."**

wiretap, a.k.a. **bug.** Perfidious secret taping of private conversations by the Nixon White House/Justice Department, denounced by Democratic investigators during the Watergate period. Not to be confused with **maintaining the historical record,** i.e., the secret taping of private conversations (including those of Martin Luther King) by the White House/Justice Department during the Kennedy-Johnson era.

woefully inadequate, a.k.a. **unacceptable!** Liberal speaker's description of Conservative administration's approach to **nagging problem,** for which he recommends a **proactive response.**

world opinion. Liberal U.S. president's inhibitor before pursuing any new foreign policy venture, i.e., What will the *Manchester Guardian* think? Note also **hearts and minds** as well as **the Arab Street**.

World's Greatest Deliberative Body. The United States Senate when fulfilling its constitutional duty to deter the **extremist** agenda of a reactionary Republican White House by means of extended debate; as distinct from **A Little Group of Willful Men,** i.e., narrow-gauged Republican obstructionists who block passage of enlightened Liberal legislation by means of Senate filibuster.

X

xenophobe. Pat Buchanan after being short-changed at a Taco Bell.

xtremist. Depending on Hillary Clinton's mood on a given Senate morning, any member of the Vast Rightwing Conspiracy to the Right of (a) Kay Bailey Hutcheson, (b) Arnold Schwarzenegger, (c) Barbara Bush.

xtraterrestrials. Formerly space aliens, but in multi-cultural Liberwock parlance, **undocumented celestial visitors.** See Oakland Mayor Jerry Brown's classic monograph, *Little Green Cards for Little Green Men* (Nebular Press).

Y

yahoos. Red-state Bush voters, presidential election of 2000; otherwise, in prospect of their going to the polls again in 2004, Heartland Americans who exalt the American Dream.

The Young, the Black, and the Poor. Prevailing Liberal campaign Trinity during the Clinton-Gore years, supplanting previous Democratic appeals to **The Common Man**—a gender-insensitive term popularized by FDR's hyper-Liberal vice president Henry Wallace in a 1942 speech, "The Century of the Common Man." Not that the Clinton-Gore model doesn't have its own insensitivity problems, beginning with **Black** (either **People of Color** or **African American** preferred) up to and including **Poor** (**Underprivileged** or **Disadvantaged** preferred, as in "For the disadvantaged you have always with you," John 12:8, New Revised Liberal Bible).

yuppies. Thirty-something urban Americans seduced by Wall Street, Madison Avenue, and the baneful specter of Lee Atwater to forsake the Liberal tradition of their Democratic parents in pursuit of Armani suits, Ferragamo shoes, and Gold Card membership in the George Bush Pioneer Club.

Z

zealot. Ralph Nader, spoiler candidate for president (2000-2004). Not to be confused with Ralph Nader, selfless consumer advocate (1965-1999).

zigzag. Erstwhile hockey jock John Kerry playing the puck of public policy in the United States Senate, 1985-2004.

ZEITGEIST: liberal-spirit-of-the-times

"I didn't even know her last name until we went to La Maze class."

—FORMER CAROLINA PANTHER RAE CARRUTH, CHARGED
WITH THE MURDER OF HIS PREGNANT GIRLFRIEND, RE HIS
PRIOR RELATIONSHIP WITH THE DECEASED.

LAST WORDS

SO YOU'VE READ BERNARD GOLDBERG ON
mainstream media bias as well as Ann Coulter on
slander and think you know all there is to know about
the way Liberals distort the news.

Well, think again. All you really know is the grand
torque of the Liberal spin machine as it goes about its
daily grind of deciding what news is or isn't fit to
print or broadcast.

In short, the Big Picture . . .

END OF WORLD IMMINENT
Low-Income Minorities Will Be Hardest Hit

—UNDATED HEADLINE, *WASHINGTON POST*

On the heels of this late-breaking story, CBS has
learned that despite being forewarned by
Gabriel's trumpet-blast, the Bush White House
has no plans to reverse what Democratic Senate
leader Tom Daschle has aptly called, I quote, its
"reckless, irresponsible policy of giving obscene
tax breaks to its rich contributor friends . . ."

—*CBS EVENING NEWS*, DAN RATHER
REPORTING, SAME DAY

That kind of frontal bias you can see coming a mile away. Not so the news warp slipped in under the verbal radar. Here for closers is a random sampling of frequently-used Liberal words and phrases that should set off spin alarms whenever read or heard:

Whenever the *New York Times* reports on Left-Right debates, Liberals invariably *assert* or *point out* while Conservatives merely *claim* or *allege.*

In *Washington Post* coverage, Liberals are known to *refute* or *counter* accusations while Conservatives unvaryingly *deny* or, worse yet, *stonewall* them.

Under aggressive questioning by *Newsweek* reporters, Liberals make their replies *heatedly* while Conservatives do so *huffily* (or, under extreme pressure, even *snap* or *sniff* their answers).

As *Time* magazine editors see it, Liberals who aren't ready to commit on controversial issues are simply *weighing their options,* while Conservatives in the same quandary are said to be *evasive* or *waffling.*

In any Capitol Hill showdown between free-market forces and Liberal groups, National Public Radio has it that the former retain *lobbyists* while the latter employ *spokesmen.*

When an "expert" quoted by the *New York Times* or

Washington Post is said to be *respected* or *widely recognized*, be assured he is speaking out in favor of some Liberal position; but when an "expert" quoted by the *Times* or *Post* speaks out in favor of a Conservative position, be assured he will be misquoted.

ON THIS DATE IN LIBERWOCK HISTORY

September 24, 1960: Eighteen-year-old Barbara Streisand decided to drop a vowel from her name in lieu of a blood-sacrifice to ensure John F. Kennedy's election.

INTERVIEW WITH THE LIBERWOCK

(IN WHICH THE LIBERAL VOCABULARY IS PUT TO THE TEST)

AL FRANKEN SLATED TO HOST LIBERAL NETWORK TALK SHOW

—Headline, *USA Today,* January 10, 2004

INTERVIEW TRANSCRIPT, THE AL FRANKEN SHOW/
April 10, 2004:

AL FRANKEN: With us tonight is Professor Ernst Angst, Dean of the Franz Liebnicht School of Liberal Clichéology. What brings you to the nation's capital, Professor?

PROFESSOR ANGST: Crunch time, Al. It's election year, and I'm here to give our Leftwing candidates a heads-up on how to articulate their agenda.

AF: By "heads-up" you mean—

PA: Bring 'em up to speed, so at the end of the day they're inside the loop.

AF: And if they're outside the loop?

PA: Not an option, so let's not go there. Look at the upside, ol' buddy. Better to be a Rosy Scenario who smells the coffee than a prophet of gloom and doom. Speaking of which, have you heard the one about the traveling pollster and the farm-worker's daughter?

AF: No, but if it's all the same, I'd rather—

PA: Stay on message, right. Not a problem, the ball's in your court.

AF: Yeah, well, I was just going over your guidebook on Liberal fundraisers—

PA: You mean, *Dialogue for Dollars*? A good read, but a little behind the curve. Nobody in Liberal circles dialogues anymore. They interact.

AF: To do what?

PA: What else? To find a level playing field, begin the healing process.

AF: I see. And what happens when the playing field's leveled and the healing begins?

PA: Depends on what they've brought to the table, whether it's a one-cycle sound-bite, or has legs.

AF: And if it has legs?

PA: Then, as Dan Rather would say, take it to the bank. Unless, of course, you overreact, in which case—

AF: Let me guess: You're out of the mainstream.

PA: I wouldn't go that far, though it's true you'd be marginalized.

AF: And if that happens?

PA: You'd have to reorder your priorities, think outside the box.

AF: In other words, the vision thing?

PA: Exactly. Hey, are you sure you don't want to hear the one about the traveling pollster and the farm-worker's daughter?

AF: Love to, Professor, but we only have time for a few questions on—

PA: Hot-button clichés? Fire away. It's your laundry list.

AF: For openers, I'd love to hear your thoughts on expanding the economy.

PA: You mean growing the economy. We expand our horizons. That's a no-brainer.

AF: As opposed to a—

PA: Non-starter, which is what comes down when you push the panic-button on a judgment call.

AF: In which event—

PA: You're in a no-win situation. You have to revisit the problem or—

AF: Let me guess—deep-six it?

PA: You're showing your age, Al. That one's out of the Watergate era. We don't deep-six things these days, we're into transparency.

AF: Which means you have to—

PA: Raise your game, get a handle on your parameters. But let's not go there because, let's face it, if we don't do it, who will?

AF: Good question, Professor. Let's see, have we left anything out?

PA: As a matter of fact, we haven't covered chilling effect or its cousin robust response, not to mention meaningful reform. But I give it a pass, in a heartbeat, because—

AF: Sorry, Professor, we've run out of time.

PA: Perfecto. Just what I've been looking for to make my day.

AF: What's that?

PA: Closure, ol' buddy, closure.

(WITH APOLOGIES TO THE LATE FRANK SULLIVAN
AND THE GREAT MR. ARBUTHNOT)

APPENDIX 2

DEAR DR. LIBERWOCK

IN WHICH THE ELDER SAGE OF LIBERALISM COUNSELS AND CONSOLES THE POLITICALLY LOVELORN

DEAR DR. LIBUTHNOT,

I am a 20-year-old sociology major at Cal
Berkeley and have fallen madly in love
with an Orange County stockbroker who
attended Pepperdine. We are serious enough
to be talking about a lifetime commitment,
but my Woodstock Liberal parents have
drawn the line over my entering into a
mixed marriage, which by their definition
means tying the knot with Larry (that's his
name), who says it's no problem because,
if necessary, he will switch his voter regis-
tration from Schwarzenegger Republican to
Democrat, Green, whatever will make my
parents happy. Knowing you are the Elder
Sage of Liberalism, I am interested in
knowing what you think. Should I take the
plunge with Larry or break it off until the
right, or as my mother says, the Left man
comes along?

—Conflicted Kim

DEAR CONFLICTED KIM,

Much as I believe in young folks throwing
off the coercive shackles of progenitive
authority, in this case I think your parents
have a point. As Elder Sage for lo these
many years, I believe the odd coupling of
James Carville and Mary Matalin has produced a misperception on the part of many
that a heartfelt Leftwinger and pathological
Reaganite can meet, mate, and live happily-
ever-after.

Not so. With rare exceptions, political
mixed marriages end up in divorce court or
anger management counseling after heated
arguments over Alger Hiss (who was inno-
cent), the Rosenbergs (who were framed),
Hiroshima (which was unnecessary), General
Custer (who had it coming), Bill Clinton (who
didn't), and/or Rush Limbaugh (a Munich
braumeister in a former life).

Is there a chance you and your benighted

Orange County stockbroker can beat those odds? Only if his promise to convert goes beyond the one-stop simplism of abandoning the Terminator and switching parties. Would he, for example, take time away from his daily grind of puts-and-calls to enroll at one of the many curative facilities springing up around the country as backlash to the Great Bush Steal of 2000? If so, my personal recommendation would be the six-week seminar now being offered by the Eleanor Roosevelt Institute for Political Correction, a remedial school best-known for having eased the transition of young Hillary Rodham from placard-carrying Goldwater Girl in the sixties to card-carrying McGovernite in the seventies.

All things considered, I think your Woodstock Liberal parents would agree.

—Dr. L.

DEAR DR. L.,

As a sophisticated New York Liberal I thought I had seen and heard it all, but a fly has landed in the ointment of my home life that baffles not only me but also two separate (and expensive) uptown marriage counselors: My wife, the mother of three, a Wellesley graduate (upper ten percent), and altogether a woman with both feet on *terra firma*, has, it seems, developed an irrepressible crush on Senator Chuck Schumer.

How irrepressible? Let me put it this way: Dora (her name) considers Schumer "a sexpot" (her words, not mine), and whenever we have a disagreement over anything, threatens to leave home and "run off with my divine Chuckie."

Any suggestions? Even her $400-an-hour therapist has given up.

—Baffled Manhattanite

DEAR BAFFLED,

It's obvious your Dora has never actually met Senator Schumer. My suggestion is that you drop the therapist, put the money saved into a Schumer fundraiser, and give your wife an opportunity to see and hear her "divine Chuckie" firsthand. If that doesn't solve your problem, nothing will.

—Dr. L.

DEAR DR. LIBUTHNOT,

You may recall that you saved my marriage a few years back when my wife and I had serious political differences over the meaning of the word "is." You advised at the time that I seek spiritual guidance from the Rev. Jesse Jackson and part my hair differently, all of which seemed to work until I retired and she decided she wanted a career of her own. Now she's getting all the attention, people think of me as a has-been, and I can't even get a reservation at a good restaurant when I want it. Tell me, Doctor, what should I do?

—Arkansas Traveler

DEAR ARKANSAS TRAVELER,

Three things: First, seek spiritual guidance from the Rev. Jesse Jackson; second, part your hair differently; third, try making the reservations in your wife's name.

—Dr. L.

APPENDIX 3

HILLARY CLINTON'S (SECRET) DIARY 1993–2001

> "I am not the sort of person who routinely pours out her deepest feelings, even to my closest friends."
>
> —HILLARY RODHAM CLINTON, LIVING HISTORY, PAGE 478

FOR EIGHT YEARS, AGAINST HER BETTER JUDGMENT, Hillary Rodham Clinton (hereinafter HRC) kept a private journal to "pour out her feelings"—a diary so personal that no one, least of all her husband, was ever allowed to see. Inspiration for this journal came from the former First Lady's friend Linda Bloodworth-Thomason*, a Hollywood producer who, she later confessed, was thinking in terms of future use of the material for an inside-the-White-House film script.

"Much as I value Linda's advice, in this case I rejected it out-of-hand," HRC would later write. "All my instincts, not to mention my legal training, argued against leaving a paper trail of words and thoughts which, in the wrong hands, could come back to haunt me."

Only after learning that her idol and role model Eleanor Roosevelt had kept a diary during her White House years

---

*Hereinafter LB-T. Other code names used in the diary include Big Shot (a.k.a. BS), Hillary's personal reference to her husband; Chel, re daughter Chelsea; Stiletto, re journalist friend Sidney Blumenthal; Hatchet, re James Carville; Mono, re Monica Lewinsky; Barbie Doll (a.k.a. Ms. Maliboob), re Barbra Streisand; Empty Suit re Vice President Al Gore; and Torquemada, re Independent Counsel Kenneth Starr.

did HRC begin "jotting notes to myself, a habit that became a ritual when I discovered that given the [expletive deleted] frustrations* that go with living in this place, letting it all out at the end of every day had certain therapeutic benefits."

Not that HRC completely lost her inhibition about the risks involved in "letting it all out." Presciently anticipating future problems with grand juries, she took to viewing her ritual jottings as "legal memoranda" immune to subpoena, so that when later asked by Independent Counsel Kenneth Starr whether she kept "a diary or personal journal," she could answer (truthfully by her lights), "No, none."

Ironically, it was this very perception of diary-keeping as "therapy" that would lead to HRC's carelessness in leaving the journal on a living-room coffee table in the Clintons' last-minute move from the White House (January 20, 2001).▲ Discovered by a member of the First Family's protective detail hours after their departure, the two-volume diary was routinely passed on to Secret Service headquarters in the Old Executive Office Building, where it remained

---

*It was no doubt due to these "frustrations" that HRC made occasional use of expressions which squeamish readers might find unbefitting her position as First Lady. All interests considered, a light censorial touch has therefore been applied to the more colorful of these phrases.—Ed.

▲Last-minute, according to former Clinton staffers, because Bill Clinton clung to the forlorn hope that the legal tie-up in the Bush-Gore election would result in his remaining in the White House beyond the constitutional 1/20/01 evacuation date. "It was surreal," said one ex-staffer. "He just didn't want to leave the place."

until, on February 9, the former First Lady inquired as to its whereabouts. Located in what the Service refers to as its "cold storage" vault, the diary was then forwarded to the Clintons' temporary residence in Little Rock—but not before copies had been made by agency personnel who over the years had been on the receiving end of HRC's frequent personal tirades against what she called "police-state goons."

Three copies were made in all. Two remain unaccounted for, but one fortunately made it into the hands of Ellis V. Cruse, curator of the Rutherford B. Hayes Center for White House Memorabilia (Ohio University). Though restrictions were placed on publication of some parts of the diary, what follows are selected excerpts from the former First Lady's private journal, available courtesy the Center and its editorial auxiliary, Tilden Press.

HILLARY AND HOLLYWOOD

Among the surprise revelations coming out of HRC's diary is the fact that, aside from the Thomasons and Arkansas-born Mary Steenburgen, the former First Lady harbored an intense dislike of what she called "the intellectual cretins" who made up her husband's political fan club in the Hollywood community. Especially irksome, as her September 12, 1992, entry indicates, were the frequent overnight stays in the Lincoln Room made by Barbra Streisand:

Barbie Doll is back in town, her third incidental drop-in since the first of the year. What a harebrain. At dinner last night she pitched her latest clownsuit scenario, this one having to do with Middle East peace: She thinks Big Shot should send an "international" figure, in this case Omar Sharif, to Jerusalem to mediate a "blockbuster" summit conference between the Israelis and the Arabs. BS not only kept a straight face but even managed to mumble something about giving it some thought, though I doubt he digested the idea in full, distracted as he was by Ms. Maliboob's low-cut cleavage . . .

JR and "THE STRANGULATOR"

The Republican takeover of Capitol Hill in November 1994 had its personal as well as political repercussions in the

Clinton White House. Staff members quickly divided into two factions—Bill's appointees versus Hillary's—with each blaming the other for losing the Senate and House. HRC's diary reveals the post-campaign argument that came out of the president's insistence on calling in guru Dick Morris for a "political fix" after what he termed "Hillary's healthcare [expletive]-up." For her part, HRC resented her husband's hiring Morris, whom she first called "Motormouth," then "The Strangulator," her expression of contempt for Morris's outside-the-box theory of political "Triangulation." On February 11, 1995, after a heated White House strategy session that ran late into the night, Hillary the diarist made the following entry into her daily journal:

Just what I needed after three hours of listening to Motormouth Morris's cockamamie theory of "Triangulation"— an [Expletive deleted] midnight call from my worst mistake, (JR!). . . Morris thinks Big Shot's best political strategy is to place himself halfway between the Gingrich crowd of crypto-fascists and what he calls

Attorney General Janet Reno

"the super-Lib" members of the Democratic Left. Super-Lib? I'd wonder who he meant except for the fact that every time he used the term he'd cut his eyes my way! Low point for the day. Or so I thought until the call came in from JR, complaining about how Web was interfering with her operation. Dimwit! She still doesn't get it. That's why Web's there! Bad as things are, God help us if Reno is left on her own . . .

Webster Hubbell, No. 2 man at Justice

ADVICE FROM ELEANOR

Hillary knew—not only about her faithless husband's affair with Monica Lewinsky but all his various extramarital affairs (forty-seven, by diary count), dating back to his days as Arkansas Attorney General. That should come as no surprise to political cynics in Washington and Little Rock, but what the former First Lady's diary reveals for the first time is her personal fury at having to "face the world not once, not twice, but again and again looking like a woman not only duped but stupid."

The journal details heated arguments in the residential quarters of the White House, verifying (in one case) the rumor that HRC had thrown a priceless Wedgwood vase at her husband. ("Nothing I'm ashamed of," she tells her diary, "other than the fact that I missed the [expletive deleted].") Her private solace? Neither the comfort of a personal minister (à la Bill's moral counsel, Jesse Jackson) nor the shoulder of a personal friend. Instead she would "commune with Eleanor" on late nights, via the full-length portrait of Mrs. Roosevelt hanging in a quiet White House corridor . . .

Excerpt, conversation between Hillary Rodham Clinton and Eleanor Roosevelt, as recorded in HRC'S daily journal, August 21, 1998:

. . . It had slipped my mind that Eleanor had her own problem with a philandering husband until she lowered her voice and, as if whispering into my good ear, said, "You're not the first, Hillary my dear, and men being men, you won't be the last." Of course, I pointed out, there's a difference between being married to a one-woman womanizer like FDR and my serial philanderer, but it all comes down to what the two-timed wife does (or threatens to do) about it. "Divorce," as Eleanor said, "is out of the question," not only for Chel's sake but my own. I split and a year from now he's still in the White House, but where would I be? A has-been First Lady who can't even get Geraldo Rivera to return her calls. "Separate beds," was Eleanor's parting advice, "not separate lives. We must never let the ████████████s off that easy." Amazing woman. I had never heard her use language like that before. Or could it all have been my imagination?

Expletive deleted

THE FINAL DAYS

A Clinton dynasty? That HRC left 1600 Pennsylvania Avenue harboring thoughts of one day returning in her own right was apparent in the final entry of her White House diary, replete with cutting references to the man she saw as a future rival:

January 19, 2001

Packing. Trying to separate the gifts we can keep outright from those we slip out the back door, when guess who finally drops by for a meeting in the Oval Office? Empty Suit himself, with bags under his watery eyes and stubble on his weak chin, as if he's had a bad night sleeping. Which he should, given the fact that we laid it all out for him, cake on a plate, and he somehow managed to get more votes than his opponent and still lose the election! I'd have thought he'd come in contrite but no, not this Mama's Boy. The way he sees it, blowing Florida and even losing his home state, is all our fault! That, from a hypocritical ingrate who went out of his way to keep anything remotely named Clinton out of his campaign. Oh well. It's all to the good because now we can't be blamed for putting George II in the White House for four, maybe even eight years, depending on what the future holds for the country and Yours Truly . . .

Getting late, very late. Ten more hours and we're out of here, into the dustbin of history. Yeah, right . . . Don't Starr, Murdoch, Limbaugh, and all those other ▬▬▬▬▬▬ s just wish!

Expletive deleted

SIX LIBERAL MYTHS

MYTH #1: The Republican Party is the racist party, Democrats are the party of civil rights and racial equality.

REALITY: Judging by the media furor raised during the presidential campaign of 2000, you'd think it was Republicans, not Democrats, who first hoisted the Confederate flag over the state house in Columbia, South Carolina.

The only issue reporters seemed interested in during that year's South Carolina Republican primary was the flag issue: How did George W. Bush and John McCain feel about the Stars and Bars over the capitol?

Odd. The Confederate flag had been flying over the South Carolina capitol for thirty-eight years, through ten presidential elections. But in all that time this question had never been asked of any presidential candidate, Democrat or Republican. Not even of South Carolina Senator Fritz Hollings when he ran for president in 1992. Why not? Hollings, after all, was the South Carolina governor who first raised the Confederate flag in 1962, as a gesture of racist defiance against federal court orders to desegregate Southern schools.

Hollings, Alabama Governor George Wallace, Mississippi Governor Ross Barnett—they were three of a kind in those early years of the civil rights struggle in the South. Democrats all, standing up for the racist principle of, as Wallace put it, "Segregation today, segregation tomorrow, segregation forever."

And what did John F. Kennedy, the Democrat then in the White House, have to say about it? Did he denounce Wallace or ask Hollings to take down the flag? Of course not. If Kennedy had, it might have alienated those Southern Democratic voters he and Lyndon Johnson needed when they ran for reelection in 1964.

Call it Kennedy's Southern strategy—the same electoral strategy the national Democratic Party had been using to hold onto the Solid South, with all its racist institutions, since 1870. Not that the Liberal media chose to label it that. On the contrary, the fact that Democratic presidents from Wilson (an avowed segregationist) to Kennedy were elected by appealing to Southern segregationist voters passed without media comment, much less censure.

Only when Republicans began competing for Southern votes in the 1960s did the moral antennae of reporters on the national scene begin to vibrate. Only then did the term "Southern strategy" take life, flourishing through four decades until, by year 2003, Democrats like Howard Dean—the New England doctor with a Liberal cure for all the nation's ills—were using it as a partisan bludgeon. For instance, here's Dean, addressing a black church audience in South Carolina, December 2003:

> In 1968 Richard Nixon won the White House. He did it in a shameful way: by dividing Americans against one another, stirring up prejudices and bringing out the worst in people. They called it the Southern strategy, and the Republicans have been using it ever since.

Conceded, Dr. Dean delivered that diatribe while in a political sweat, struggling to regain lost ground with black voters. A few weeks earlier, the former Vermont governor had put his left foot in his mouth by urging the Democratic Party to go after the votes of "people who drive pickup trucks with Confederate flags."

In short, adopt a Southern strategy. Or does that take Dr. Dean's overheated statement out of context? Hard to tell. Like most Liberals called on to deal with the past, Howard Dean has a gift for fiction and a pliable memory. A refresher course is in order, not only for Liberal politicians but also for those mainstream journalists who, because of selective amnesia or stunted progressive education, foster the myth that the Democratic Party is the party of civil rights and racial equality:

Jim Crow laws were the spawn and legacy of Southern Democrats, protected for the better part of a century by the acquiescence of enabling Democratic presidents unwilling to antagonize their political base.

The Civil Rights Act of 1964 would never have passed—according to no less an authority than Lyndon Johnson—without the help of Republican leaders like Illinois Senator Everett Dirksen and Ohio Congressman William McCullough. (Among those Southern Democrats voting against the 1964 Civil Rights Bill were, notably, Bill Clinton's Arkansas mentor, Senator William Fulbright, and Al Gore's father, Tennessee Senator Albert Gore.)

Despite Harry Truman's promise to black voters during the 1948 presidential election, he left the White House in January 1953 with the Nation's Capital still a segregated city. It took a Republican president, Dwight Eisenhower, to desegregate the District of Columbia—the same Dwight Eisenhower who in 1957 dispatched the 101st Airborne Division to Little Rock to escort black students into Central High School after Democratic Governor Orval Faubus blocked a federal integration order.

Three years later, in the presidential election of 1960, the Kennedy-Johnson ticket swept the South by charging Ike's vice president with being part of a Republican administration that "forced integration on the people of Little Rock at the point of a bayonet."

Southern strategy? Richard Nixon learned everything he needed to know about it in Arkansas.

MYTH #2: Richard Nixon was an anti-Semite.

REALITY: I know, I know . . . it's all there on the tapes and in the transcripts: Nixon in the Oval Office, fulminating about Jews in politics, Jews in the media . . . but did that make him an anti-Semite or simply a man given to venting ethnic slurs he wouldn't utter in polite company?

Let's put it this way: Have you ever heard it said that Harry Truman was an anti-Semite? I thought not. Yet here's what historian Michael Beschloss says in his book, *The Conquerors*: "Truman was prone in private to use crude anti-Semitic language that belied his growth as a national figure."

Such as? "To the private Truman," writes Beschloss, "New York City was 'Kike-town' and greedy poker players 'screamed like Jewish merchants'—this, despite the fact that one such merchant, Eddie Jacobson, was his old haberdashery partner in Kansas City and a lifelong friend."

And more: Asked whether Treasury Secretary Henry Morgenthau would accompany him to a summit with Churchill and Stalin in the spring of 1945, Truman replied, "Neither Morgenthau nor [Bernard] Baruch nor any of the Jew boys will be going to Potsdam"; after which he testily wrote in his diary, "The Jews claim God Almighty picked 'em out for special privilege, [but] I'm sure he had better judgment."

Still, writes Beschloss, Truman's private comments had no bearing on his public policy toward Jews or the state of Israel. "As a senator, he was ahead of Roosevelt in speaking out against Hitler's war on Jews, and as president he overruled his own State Department in recognizing Israel in 1948."

The same can be said (though it's not likely that his Liberal detractors will say it) of Richard Nixon, still remembered in Jerusalem and Tel Aviv as one of Israel's staunchest supporters. Not to mention, on the personal front, the array of Jewish friends and advisors who filled Nixon's life and career from his early days as a congressman to his final days as president: Murray Chotiner, Max Rabb, Henry Kissinger, Bill Safire, Herbert Stein, Leonard Garment . . .

No, Liberal myth to the contrary, Richard Nixon was not an anti-Semite. But he would have done well to take John Connally's advice and burned those tapes.

MYTH #3: Despite all the calumnies heaped on him, Bill Clinton left office as a popular president who could have been elected to a third term if the Constitution allowed it.

REALITY: If you haven't heard this one, come to Washington and strike up a conversation with a Liberal

Democrat about the 2000 election. After he or she gets past the expletives about Florida's having been stolen, the storyline becomes one of might-have-beens: how, if he'd had the chance, charismatic Bill could would have been swept into office for a third term.

Don't laugh. Liberal Democrats seriously believe this. And given the ever-ready help of Leftwing historians, don't be surprised if, after memories of Monica have faded, there comes a revisionist attempt to upgrade the Clinton presidency in the Judgment of History.

But third term? Remind whatever Clintonite who tries to push this line that their charismatic leader in two campaigns never drew more than 43 percent of the presidential vote. Al Gore couldn't carry his home state, but even he did better than that.

MYTH #4: Whatever your opinion of Jimmy Carter's presidency, he's emerged in his post-presidential years as a great elder statesman.

REALITY: Give the Leftwing revisionists credit—they never give up trying to turn their lemons into lemonade or, in Lyndon Johnson's more pungent phrase, their chicken-bleep into chicken salad.

Recession, inflation, Teheran. What else is there to say about Jimmy Carter's four years in the White House? Oh, yes, let's not forget—malaise. Which leaves Carter's apologists no option but to argue the virtues of their hero's ex-presidency.

First, they say, there's the work Jimmy puts into Habitat for Humanity. Commendable work, and if they stopped there they might make the case that Carter is indeed a unique ex-president, an exemplar for a golf-playing, banquet-circuit breed. But they don't stop there and, unfortunately, neither does he.

From the day Jimmy Carter left the White House, he let it be known that he still saw himself as a world leader, anointed to resolve all differences between continents, nations, and tribes. His talent unaccountably unsought during the Reagan years, Carter settled on simply writing nonbooks and traveling the globe to denigrate U.S. foreign policy to any reporter with a pen and tape recorder.

Then came Bill Clinton, a president so disengaged from foreign affairs (as opposed to the domestic variety) that an ex-president's standing offer to serve as a global troubleshooter was irresistible. Wasn't this, after all, the peacemaker who brokered the Camp David accord between Egypt and Israel?

The problem was—and is—that like virtually every public issue Jimmy Carter puts his healing touch to, the Camp David accord proved to be less than met the camera's eye. Camp David promised, according to the hyped press releases issuing from the White House, to be a harbinger of peace throughout the Middle East. Try selling that on the streets of Cairo or Jerusalem a quarter-century later.

Or try selling the virtue of Carter diplomacy on the streets of Port-au-Prince today. There, in 1995, Jimmy (with his usual fanfare) helped leverage the tinhorn dictator Jean-Baptiste Aristide back into power in the name of democracy and human rights. This, fresh from Carter's peacemaking triumph in Pyongyang where, with the help of Secretary of State Madeleine Albright (who did a dance for the cameras to celebrate the occasion), the ex-president negotiated a "Framework" for North Korea to dismantle its nuclear weapons program.

Euchred again; though what more should we expect from a delusionary Georgia peanut farmer who, as president, told the world that he relied on his preteen daughter for advice on nuclear matters and confessed that he hadn't truly understood the nature of Soviet Communism until Russian troops marched into Afghanistan?

MYTH #5: The Cuban missile crisis of October 1962 brought the world to the brink of World War III, but ended with an historic American victory in the Cold War.

REALITY: Had it been a Republican president there would have been dark insinuations that he'd planned it all as an October Surprise. For months New York Senator Kenneth Keating had been warning that the Russians were building a missile base in Castro's Cuba—warnings dismissed by the Kennedy White House as the partisan railing of a paranoid Republican.

Then, suddenly, a change in stories: Only a few weeks before the midterm congressional elections, the president cancels a speech in Chicago to return to Washington and report that yes, the Russians are indeed building a missile base in Cuba and he's ordered the U.S. Navy to interdict all Soviet supply ships headed for Havana.

High point for the Kennedy presidency after a series of low points—the Bay of Pigs, the construction of the Berlin Wall, the Vienna summit with Nikita Khrushchev where Kennedy appears unsure of himself and ripe for bullying.

Predictably Khrushchev, both a bully and a gambler, goes forward with a high-risk plan to construct a Soviet missile site in Cuba—an overreach that puts the world's two great superpowers on a collision course to all-out war.

Or does it? Forty years of Liberal histo-fiction would have us believe that only the Kennedys' deft leadership (Bobby's role is part of the myth) saved the world from a nuclear autumn. So at least say such biased eyewitnesses as Robert McNamara and Arthur Schlesinger Jr. But to believe this docu-dramatic tale of civilization-on-the-brink, you also have to buy into a scenario in which Khrushchev manages to persuade the ruling Politburo that defending Cuba is worth the risk of mushroooom clouds over Moscow and Leningrad. ("After all, Comrades, we gave Fidel our word!")

So much for the McNamara-Schlesinger myth of Armageddon averted. But cosmic crisis or no, didn't the Cuban missile face-off end with a Cold War victory for the United States and a humiliating setback for the Soviet Union?

That, to paraphrase the parsing of a latter-day Liberwock, all depends on the meaning of the word "victory." Consider: for years, dating back to the Stalin era, the Soviets had demanded the removal of U.S. missile bases in Turkey—to no avail. But six months after the Russians abandoned their missile venture in the Caribbean, all U.S. bases in Turkey were closed down.

Was it a quid-pro-quo for Khrushchev's hasty retreat? "Rightwing screed," snapped McNamara's Pentagon: "We made no deal." Though with the passage of time and the slow lift of Camelot fog, it's clear that that's precisely what it was—not a Cold War victory for the United States but an October tradeoff for the Kennedy White House.

MYTH #6: The Watergate break-in of June 1972 was part of a massive Nixonian plot to subvert the Constitution and establish a police state.

REALITY: Conceded, the Watergate break-in wasn't exactly the "third-rate burglary" that the Nixon press office derisively called it; but neither was it the Seven-Days-in-May scenario the Liberal press would have us believe. As Victor Lasky pointed out in his book, *It Didn't Start with Watergate*, there were break-ins, wire-taps, down-and-dirty activities carried out by prior administrations, from Franklin Roosevelt's to Lyndon Johnson's.

Not that Senator Sam Ervin's 1973–74 Watergate Committee was initially interested in looking into those past transgressions. Only when pushed did Ervin's investigators begin delving into such pre-Watergate conduct as Johnson's no-holds-barred FBI and IRS harassment of his political opponents and critics.

How bad were LBJ's extra-legal activities? Even a Nixon-phobe like the *New York Times*' Tom Wicker had to conclude, after going over investigators' files, that they "lend credence to Senator Goldwater's belief that, as Mr. Johnson's Republican opponent, he was wiretapped in 1964; and to Mr. Nixon's charge that when he was running against Hubert Humphrey in 1968, Mr. Johnson—still in the White House—eavesdropped on the Republican candidates."

With that as background, the question is why, thirty years after the fact, the myth of Watergate as an unprecedented

White House putsch lives on? Could it be—just one Conservative cynic's guess—that as an enduring tale of political morality it's made (and continues to make) so many Liberal journalists and writers on both coasts rich-and-famous?

Whatever the reason, the fact that the Republic founded by Washington, Jefferson, Hamilton, and Franklin wasn't really saved by Woodward, Bernstein, Redford, and Hoffman has, for all practical purposes, become irrelevant. The old John Ford line would seem to apply here: Given a choice between fact and legend, Liberals prefer to print the legend.

APPENDIX 5

REFLECTIONS OF AN EX-LIBERWOCK

> "There's no use trying," she said: "One can't believe impossible things."
>
> "I daresay you haven't had much practice," said the Queen. "When I was your age, I always did it for half-an-hour a day. Why, sometimes I've believed as many as six impossible things before breakfast."
>
> —THROUGH THE LOOKING GLASS

. . . .

> "Ich bin ein Berliner!"
>
> —JOHN F. KENNEDY, WEST BERLIN, JUNE 26, 1963

BEWARE THE LIBERWOCK, MY SON. ESPECIALLY ONE who makes great speeches: Franklin Roosevelt, Adlai Stevenson, John F. Kennedy—all the spellbinders of my youth were men with a gift for words.

For fiction, too, but that insight would come only later, about the time the Liberwock-in-chief was being cheered for that speech in Berlin, a city divided because two years earlier he'd stood by and done nothing while Nikita Khrushchev put up the Wall.

It would be a reprise of his Miami speech, in the spring of 1961, when he'd traveled south to explain (or paper over) his failure to take action while Fidel Castro was rounding up

Cuban freedom fighters at the Bay of Pigs. They cheered him there, too.

"I am a Berliner! . . . Cuba libre!"

Empty phrases, but all was forgiven. A fawning media called it the Kennedy charisma. Whatever it was, the man who possessed it marveled at his own power. "It's amazing," he would tell his brother Bobby. "The worse we do, the more popular I get."

IF YOU BELIEVE

Along with other self-defined visionaries of my generation, I had voted for Kennedy in 1960, convinced by Liberwock logic that anyone who could quote Origen, T.S. Eliot, George Bernard Shaw, and Barbara Tuchman in the course of a twenty-minute speech had to know something about running a country. Not that there wasn't more in John F. Kennedy's arsenal of promise than his ability to out-quote Richard Nixon.

John Kenneth Galbraith, the Delphic oracle of Liberwock pundits, gave testimony to Kennedy's *vision*. Norman Mailer and Gore Vidal, for all their differences, were as one about his *gravitas*. Arthur Schlesinger Jr. wrote that after eight years of Republican darkness the genie of History had sent America a beacon to light the way.

Elect this Liberwock, we were told, and he would rescue

the economy, bridge the racial gulf, close the missile gap, eliminate Castro, call Khrushchev's bluff, and last but not least, "get America moving again."

Six impossible things before breakfast. It was amazing, all right; but by 1964 the less visionary among us had stopped believing.

LEFT BEHIND

Ronald Reagan used to tell the story of his switch in political allegiance, Democrat to Republican. I didn't leave the Democratic Party, he'd explain, the Democratic Party left me: First, there was the split brought on when his Left Coast colleagues objected to his outspoken stand against Communists in the film industry; then, over a period of years, a growing recognition that the term "Liberal" as he once understood it no longer meant *liberal*.

Still, converting from Roosevelt (or in my case Kennedy) Democrat to Goldwater Republican was quite a political switch. What was it about Barry Goldwater that brought in converts? There was the book, yes, *The Conscience of a Conservative*. But it wasn't as if Goldwater were the first Conservative in public life to spell out a philosophy of governance.

What then? His gift for eloquence, the spellbinder's touch? Hardly. If Barry Goldwater had a gift, a beacon to light the way for nascent Conservatives in the volatile sixties, it was his genius for straight talk, blunt and unvarnished. In fact, political legend has it that the most eloquent speech to come out of the Republican presidential campaign of 1964 was delivered not by the candidate but the convert, Ronald Reagan.

He was the Liberwocks' worst nightmare—a spellbinder who thought like Goldwater but spoke like Kennedy.

BEYOND THE LOOKING-GLASS

"Mr. Gorbechev, tear down this wall!"

—RONALD REAGAN, WEST BERLIN, JUNE 17, 1987

They winced when he called it the "Evil Empire," not so much because he said it as because he *meant* it. Rightwing extremism. Amiable duncery. Words scrawled by a crayon-using B-movie actor on a Hollywood cue-card.

Reagan get credit for winning the Cold War? Don't be simplistic. The Nobel Liberwocks said it all when they awarded their prize to Gorbachev. The *New York Times* and *Washington Post*, Peter Jennings and NPR, Harvard, Berkeley, and People for the American Way all agreed that the fall of the Soviet Union had nothing to do with SDI and Reykjavik but came about solely because of inner contradictions and macro-dynamic pressures in a command economy.

But it would take Bill Clinton's Strobe Talbott—his Oxford roomie and foremost expert on Russian affairs—to bring it all home in the refracted style of a churlish guest at the Mad Hatter's Tea Party: Not only did Reagan have nothing to do with the Soviet breakup, said Talbott, but he and his delusional friends had it wrong from the start: There *never was* a Communist threat. It only existed in the twisted minds of Rightwing paranoids!

Which brings us, I do believe, back where we started. Liberals: If you don't take them seriously, they can be a load of laughs.